THE SEARCH

A BIOGRAPHY OF LEO TOLSTOY

ILLUSTRATIONS BY STEPHEN GAMMELL

THE SEARCH

A BIOGRAPHY OF LEO TOLSTOY

BY SARA NEWTON CARROLL

HARPER & ROW, PUBLISHERS

NEW YORK, EVANSTON, SAN FRANCISCO, LONDON

FIRST EDITION

"I have loved truth more than anything; and I do not despair of finding it, but I am still searching and searching. . . . But I'm alone, and it is hard and terrible, and it seems that I have lost my way."

From a letter to a friend when
Leo Tolstoy was almost forty

To Kells and to my mother

CONTENTS

AUTHOR'S NOTE

This biography of Tolstoy could not have been written without the richly detailed scholarship of Ernest J. Simmons, Henri Troyat, and Aylmer Maude. I am grateful to these and the other authors and translators listed in my Note on Sources for unearthing and gathering the hundreds of documents on which all study of Tolstoy's life must rest. Tolstoy cared passionately for the truth, and I, in my turn, have been careful to record the days of this remarkable man in factual terms. All episodes and events are taken from documented sources. All dialogues and quotations come from Tolstoy's diaries, reminiscences, correspondence, and autobiographical works, or from the diaries, correspondence, and memoirs of his family, friends, and contemporaries. Sometimes a line or two from a diary or letter has been presented as a thought or comment, but in every case both direct and indirect dialogues are based on actual conversations reported by the speakers themselves or by witnesses.

What prompts an author to choose a subject? I decided to write this biography after reading Tolstoy's Confession, *which might be called an autobiographical chapter in his life, a chapter in which he found joy after a time of deep despair. A special word of thanks must go to Dr. Carl Purinton for introducing me to Tolstoy's life and to his religious thought.*

Much is owed to a splendid institution called "Interlibrary Loan," which makes research by mail a pleasure, and the fine librarians at the University of Alabama, Florida State University, the Library of Congress, and Joint Universities Library in Nashville, Tennessee. In particular, credit for research materials is due Alice Doughtie, Lydia Parker, and the kind, excellent staff of the Dale County Library in Ozark, Alabama; Dr. Kenneth Croslin, Thelma Mershon, Betty Chancellor, Martin Kruskopf, and Harriet Venable of the Troy State University Library in Troy, Alabama; and the staff of the Houston Memorial Library in Dothan, Alabama.

I would like to acknowledge my debt to those who encouraged me to begin and to continue as a writer. Among these were my father, William Franklin Newton, and, from the faculty of Troy State University, Dr. Joseph Roberts, Dr. Gertrude Schroeder, and M. Study Slater; and, at Harper & Row, a fine editor, Elaine Edelman, who guided me along the way. To my mother, my sister, and my children, I am obliged for affectionate advice and unfailing interest. Deepest appreciation goes to my husband, Kells C. Carroll, for his assistance, sense of humor, and understanding during long months of research.

During Tolstoy's lifetime the Julian (or "old style") calendar was used in Russia; I have stayed with the Julian dates in this book. These dates were twelve days behind the Gregorian ("new style") calendar used in Europe during the nineteenth century, thirteen days behind during the twentieth century.

Sara Newton Carroll
Ozark, Alabama
March, 1973

ABOUT THE ILLUSTRATIONS

Stephen Gammell's illustrations are free renderings based on extensive research among historical documents, especially photographs of Leo Tolstoy, his family, and his home. Drawings and photographs of Russian architecture and costume made during Tolstoy's lifetime were also consulted.

THE SEARCH

A BIOGRAPHY OF LEO TOLSTOY

THE SECRET OF THE GREEN STICK

The country estate called Yasnaya Polyana, or "Clear Glade," was a delightful place for children to play. An ancient, crumbling brick wall meandered around extensive acres which nestled into rolling Russian countryside, one hundred thirty miles south of Moscow. Flowing swiftly between the hills, the deep Voronka River echoed shouts of swimmers or of young people catching crayfish in summer. Four lakes teemed with carp and froze in winter for skating. Wild game flourished in the forests of birch and larch. Nearby, many small houses made up a hamlet of serfs; serf children shyly bowed when the sons of their master, Count Nicholas Tolstoy, ran past. A drive bordered by lime trees wound past two brick guardhouses at the entrance gates and up the incline to the white-porticoed mansion house of Yasnaya Polyana; the house's many casement windows looked across wooded hills toward the old highway to Kiev. Hunting dogs loped across the grounds among the overgrown elders and ash trees. Oxen watched as the children rode their ponies past fields of corn, wheat, oats, and rye.

On this particular day, three sons of Count Tolstoy were playing in a shady ravine near the edge of a wood. Larks sang in a field near the ravine where Nicholas, the oldest, whispered to six-year-old Dmitri and to handsome Sergei, who was seven. The boys noticed their youngest brother approaching. Five-year-old Leo had only recently been allowed to explore the outdoors with his brothers, and each day uncovered new wonders: the blue Russian sky, the greening hills, white birch trees to climb, rushing streams to dam, and the hushed shadiness of this ravine near the wood. Leo hurried to join his brothers. Would they tell him what they were whispering about? A fresh forest smell filled the air. The boys gave Nicholas their worshipful attention as the older brother slowly announced a marvelous secret that would make all men happy. When the secret was revealed, he said, there would be no more quarreling, no more misfortune, no more sickness, no more anger. The marvelous secret was written on a green stick, he told them—a green stick that had been buried at the edge of the ravine in this year, 1833.

To pudgy five-year-old Leo, being included in his brothers' company and games was the beginning of a new and wonderful life. And the idea of rescuing humanity forever through a secret on a green stick overwhelmed him with a reverence more puzzling than any he had felt even at his prayers. Dimly he understood that Nicholas might allow him, Leo, some part in this great adventure. He thought he heard their tutor calling across the meadow, as he squinted in the sunlight and wondered *how* they could find the green stick with the secret written on it.

These boys were the descendants of a long line of prominent Russians of intelligence and integrity, including princes, counts, diplomats, governors, courtiers, generals, and their wives. It is true there were also among the ancestors some scheming politicians as well as extravagant gamblers, spendthrifts, and a few spoiled ladies whose every whim had been satisfied from birth to death by a multitude of servants. Portraits of these wealthy noblemen and their wives lined the walls of the large, plainly furnished rooms at Yasnaya Polyana and looked down severely from gold-leaf frames at the latest Tolstoy children, Nicholas, Sergei, Dmitri, Leo, and their little sister, Marya. Talented serfs had painted these portraits and made much of the furniture in the thirty-room house, which had been built by other serfs.

An early Count Tolstoy had been a brilliant politician of seventeenth-century Russia. As a favorite of Tsar Peter the Great, Peter Tolstoy was rewarded with lands and high positions. When his ambitious foot slipped, the Count was exiled to a cold island monastery on the White Sea. His great-grandson, Ilya Tolstoy, doubled the family fortune by marrying the daughter of a very rich prince. Count Ilya entertained generously, gambled incessantly, and indulged his luxurious tastes recklessly for years. Finally the wealth and lands were spent, and only enough influence was left to get him appointed governor of a small city on the Volga River. As the debts piled up, the governor saved the shreds of his flamboyant reputation by dying. He left his son Nicholas no money, only a household of women to look after— Nicholas' mother, a queenly woman accustomed to many servants; Alexandra, a devout sister whose husband had gone insane; and Alexandra's foster daughter, Pashenka. Another sister, Pelagya, had married and lived in Kazan. There was also a second cousin, Tatyana, who had been raised with the family. For years Tatyana had quietly idolized her dashing cousin Nicholas.

A gentleman of noble family like Nicholas Tolstoy was not expected to work for his living, but rather to accept a position at which he would seldom actually labor. During Napoleon's march on Moscow in 1812, Nicholas, at eighteen, had impulsively joined the Russian army; he had been captured by the French. Now he wanted no more of army life. Penniless and desperate after his father's death, Nicholas finally accepted the post of superintendent at the military orphanage in Moscow.

Count Nicholas Tolstoy (who was to become Leo Tolstoy's father) was a fascinating, self-contained charmer, in demand socially not only because of his famous family, but also for his air of serene self-confidence. Tender and cheerful to his mother and sister, he was probably half in love with admiring Cousin Tatyana. But everyone in the family, Tatyana included, understood that Nicholas must save them by a brilliant marriage to a wealthy girl, preferably a girl of fine family. He himself realized that a man in his circumstances must be more practical than sentimental, and so he listened when relatives in Moscow suggested an arranged marriage with homely but wealthy Princess Marya Volkonsky.

Marya had been the delight of her eccentric and autocratic father, Prince Volkonsky, the owner of vast lands and eight hundred serfs. In 1800 the aristocratic widower had retired to his secluded country estate at Yasnaya Polyana, where he enjoyed books, greenhouses, and his obedient, loving child, Marya.

But with the death of her father, Marya's world collapsed. Plain to look at, no longer young, and feeling completely alone, Marya wanted to die too. At last kind friends introduced her to suave, unprosperous Count Nicholas Tolstoy, five years her junior. When the princess married Nicholas, she married his household as well. About a year later, they moved from Moscow to the estate she had inherited, Yasnaya Polyana, bringing with them pale old Countess Tolstoy and the other women of the Tolstoy family. Cousin Tatyana stifled her jealousy and came to love Nicholas' bride.

Their first baby, Nicholas, was born June 31, 1823, and Marya's joy was complete. When he was almost three, another boy, Sergei, was born. A year later a third son, Dmitri, arrived. With the house full of servants, children seemed only pleasure to their parents. Marya resumed playing her piano. Beethoven's sonatas were among her favorites. She also began giving Italian lessons to Tatyana. After their formal dinners Nicholas would entertain the ladies with his hunting stories or gossip from Moscow. On August 28, 1828, the family welcomed another plump baby— Leo. Marya called him "my little Benjamin," and Papa named him "big Pouf." Once, Marya had thought she would live out her days a lonely old maid. Now, as the nurses brought in her children, she glowed and crossed herself.

Two years later, she was dead. She never recovered from the birth of her last child, a daughter named Marya. His wife gone, Count Nicholas felt quite lost. What would he do with five children? Pretty, affectionate cousin Tatyana came to his rescue. Bowing always to the wishes of the silver-haired Countess Tolstoy, leaving Nicholas' sister Alexandra to her religious devotions, Tatyana managed the household calmly. Her greatest concern was the children.

Leo later recalled Auntie Tatyana's kindness as he was growing up. One memorable event was his move from the upstairs nursery, which he shared with his baby sister, Marya, to the downstairs rooms of his brothers and their German tutor, Fyodor Rössel. Leo was five. Aunt Tatyana called him into her room next door to the nursery. Auntie's room smelled deliciously of dried figs and gingerbread that she kept in jars on her dresser. She put a new bathrobe on him, kissing him as she tied the cord at his waist. Leo felt very, very sad, and understood that life was no game. Then he went solemnly downstairs to live with the older boys.

One winter day the boys were playing indoors, huddled under a tent made of drawing-room chairs and scarves. A fire crackled in the tall Dutch oven in the corner. Leo pressed his oldest brother Nicholas with questions. *How* could they find the green stick with the secret that helps everyone? Nicholas regarded his three brothers soberly, as though testing the worth of each. At last he made them swear that they would never reveal the conditions to anyone. The younger boys agreed. Nicholas lowered his voice. The English piano sounded softly in another room. First, whispered Nicholas, each of them must train himself to stand in a corner and to not think about a white bear. Not think about a white bear? Dmitri looked puzzled. Then, Nicholas said, each must walk along a crack in the floorboards without wobbling. And for a whole year each of them must keep from looking at a hare—alive, dead, or even cooked! Even more difficult conditions might have to be fulfilled later, he warned. But Leo had already run to the corner of the room and was trying desperately not to think of a white bear so that he might find in the shady ravine a green stick carved with the secret of happiness for all mankind.

YASNAYA POLYANA

Although his brother Nicholas seemed wise and good, and deserving of deep respect, it was handsome Sergei whom Leo imitated and adored. Nicholas read constantly and did not like to be disturbed. Leo dismissed quiet Dmitri as being too near his own age to admire. But Sergei was a hero. He was always singing, inventing interesting activities, and exhibiting perfect self-confidence. When Sergei acquired gray tufted chickens to raise, Leo demanded similar pets and fed them exactly as his older brother did.

The little brother envied Sergei's casual egotism and fine appearance. Leo thought of himself as clumsy, self-conscious, and ugly. His face was a great source of dissatisfaction. He often practiced pleasant expressions in front of a mirror, praying that some miracle would improve his looks. His small gray eyes, although intelligent, seemed much too close together, and his hair bristled out in every direction. He was muscular, short, and strong, but he was awkward and very bashful. In an attempt to become handsome, he once shaved his eyebrows off completely, and then was too embarrassed to show himself in company.

Because he observed truthfulness in Sergei, Leo scorned lying.

But pretending was marvelous fun. The children improvised scenes from *The Swiss Family Robinson*, which they had read in the schoolroom. Until they were allowed to go hunting with the adults, they staged splendid hunts of their own, aiming sticks at imaginary wolves and bears. The drawing-room chairs were transformed into carriages and the tireless young travelers journeyed to Moscow, Paris, Kazan, or St. Petersburg. Little sister Marya was sometimes condescendingly included as a passenger. Nicholas was almost always the driver.

On the patterned carpet, battalions of lead soldiers were marched endlessly into heroic battle. The boys with their small armies probably dramatized Napoleon's 1812 invasion of Moscow, while Papa, a veteran of that war, watched from his chair, wreathed in a pungent circle of pipe smoke.

Sometimes, when the military maneuvers were over and the boys were alone in the room, Nicholas would again mention in a hushed voice the mystery of the green stick hidden in the shady ravine. Much of their play concluded with this dream. "We called it a game," Leo Tolstoy wrote many years later, "but really everything in the world is a game except that."

The old house rang with songs throughout the year. Encouraged by a music teacher and a dancing master, the young people practiced mazurkas and waltzes, sonatas and symphonic themes. Pashenka constantly played the piano, and, later, so did Marya and the boys. All this would have been firmly approved by Grandfather Volkonsky: In the old days at Yasnaya Polyana a full orchestra of serfs had played Haydn each morning during his breakfast.

"Go, Little Ruble" was Yuletide entertainment during which the serfs followed a tradition of surging into the master's house to receive gifts. Laughter echoed through the great hall as these familiar figures entered in disguise, their humble stations transformed intriguingly by makeshift fancy dress. The fragrance of a Christmas tree intoxicated them all while peasant women dressed as men and men dressed as women came bowing in, kissing the shoulders of the happy Tolstoy children. Leo was so filled with admiration for his painted mustache that he could hardly tear himself away from the mirror.

The house was already crowded with teachers, relatives, servants, and frequent guests, when a neighbor's child, Dunya, was taken in to be raised with the family. The shy foster daughter was five, about Leo's age. Since Leo was learning French quite rapidly, he was delegated to teach Dunya the French alphabet. The pair chose a quiet spot on the stair landing. He pointed to each letter in the primer and pronounced it proudly and precisely. *A, bé, cé*. Hesitant, the dark-eyed pupil followed his lead. *A, bé, cé*. He continued, nodding severely. *Dé, e, effe*. She responded wearily. *Dé, e, effe*. The baby professor believed in repetition. *A, bé, cé, dé, e, effe*. Dunya shook her head. *A, bé, cé, dé, e, effe!* The unhappy girl began to cry, amplifying to a shrill wail. Her exasperated teacher joined in the tears. The educator earned only reproachful looks from his new playmate, and a nickname, "Crybaby Leo," from the boys.

Thirty house servants waited on the inhabitants of the Tolstoy estate. Hundreds of other serfs worked in the fields and forests of Yasnaya Polyana. The cruel system of serfdom had existed in Russia for so many centuries that it seemed a normal way of life both to master and to serf. The nobility, the Orthodox Church, and the ruling tsars had gained a crushing legal power over these peasants, who each year found themselves deeper in debt to their masters. It was said that they were not actually slaves; many of them owned an isba (a peasant hut) and a tiny plot of land. But they themselves were also owned; their masters could buy and sell them like beasts of burden, and controlled their movements, their marriages, their entire lives.

Field serfs—muzhiks—were required to produce crops, sharing the harvest with their masters. Masters were expected to clothe and house their serfs, to provide land, money, and, in time of drought, food. There was a certain amount of stealing among serfs, and reprimands followed. Floggings were an everyday happening at many country estates, though at Yasnaya Polyana such drastic punishment was unusual.

The serfs of the field were often devoted to their master and his family, but it was the house servants who had the close relationship with them. At estates like Yasnaya Polyana, the families

9

of house servants had lived with and served their gentry for generations. The household comprised their whole world. Their responsibilities and power over other servants gave them importance and satisfaction. Since there were almost no schools, a literate serf was a great rarity, but many were intelligent and talented.

The Tolstoy house serfs were familiar and interesting characters. It was pure joy for a child to be scooped up by the butler Vasili for a ride on his big tray. Vasili's special smile tweaked one side of his face. The peculiar smell of his jacket drifted down to the other children, who squealed, "Me too! My turn!" How frightened and resentful was the young gentleman who got himself reprimanded by Praskovya, the grumpy housekeeper. Splendidly, admirably formal was Foka, the brass-buttoned majordomo, as he announced with dignity each afternoon, "Dinner is served!" Twenty years earlier, Foka had been a violinist in Grandfather Volkonsky's orchestra. The ancient footman Tikhon stood rigidly behind Grandmother's chair during dinner each night. He had played the flute long ago for the old prince's pleasure. Dusky Tatyana was the children's maid, and her brother, Nicholai, who smelled strongly of stable manure, was the soft-spoken coachman. Each of the youngsters had rested against the ample bosom of nurse Anna in infancy; she remained, grinning with only one tooth in her head. Numerous other servants hovered about. Most were fairly idle.

Religious pilgrims praying their way from monastery to monastery often stopped at Yasnaya Polyana. It was customary for estate owners to feed and shelter such people as they paused to rest. Some pilgrims wore heavy chains under their rags as a penance for sin. Aunt Alexandra was never too busy with her religious rituals to be kind to them, and the Tolstoy children were intrigued by these dingy, odorous visitors. They eavesdropped as the "holy fools" mumbled their long sad prayers.

In Aunt Tatyana's room little Leo discussed the Christ to whom these pilgrims prayed, and years later he wrote about his memory. Settling comfortably in Auntie's chair, the boy had gazed up at her icon, an image of the savior set in silver.

"Auntie, why did they torture Him?" he asked.

"They were wicked people."

"But He was good, so good! . . . Why did they beat Him? Did it hurt Him, Auntie, did it hurt Him?" To Leo, the face of Jesus in the icon seemed even sadder than the faces of the pilgrims.

Stepanovich was a barefooted pilgrim who lingered at the Tolstoy home. Each night this gifted storyteller entertained majestic Grandmother Tolstoy. Since the old man was blind, Grandmother's maid would lead him into her room, where she was preparing for bed. Often the children were allowed to take turns spending the night with her. When Leo had been baptized, Grandmother had been named his godmother, so he felt she was especially his, and that he most deserved the pleasure of visiting in her room. She made marvelous soap bubbles between her wrinkled hands as she washed, preparing for bed, smiling at the drowsy child who watched her. With the strong smell of soap in his nostrils, smoothing the embroidered bed linens under his hand, Leo was captivated by the voice of blind Stepanovich: "A certain ruling King had an only son. . . ." Sleepy Leo sank back on the down pillows in the vast snowy bed and watched the closed eyelids of the ragged peasant as the legend droned on. Stepanovich could not see Grandmother nor the wonderful soap bubbles nor Leo nor the big white bed. But he could tell splendid tales. Soon the boy's eyes would close, and the strange, solemn, monotonous stories wove themselves into his dreams.

Nothing pleased young Leo more than stories. He was reading more and more for himself. At seven he started writing a collection of his own, which he titled "Children's Amusements." It consisted mostly of short descriptions of various birds. The cock and peacock were described from nature. Owl, hummingbird, eagle, hawk, and parrot were found in Grandfather's encyclopedia. Aunt Tatyana thought Leo's work was splendid.

And Praskovya, the housekeeper, could tell marvelous, true stories about Grandfather Volkonsky. She knew all about his journey to Austria in the honor guard of Catherine the Great, Empress of All the Russias. She could tell about his orchestra, his flowers, and his inventions. She had rocked the children's mother as a baby, and the mention of Marya's name would bring tears to her shrewd old eyes. The children would sit and coax this brusque, practical woman into a warm storytelling mood. Praskovya was highly respected for her quick temper, and because she held that dread position, chief administrator of enemas to sick children.

Acting out stories and playing charades were favorite games as the children grew older. One warm day the young people were engaged in charades as they sat on the balcony outside the Italian window. An attractive girl was visiting. Lyubov Islenyev was three years older than Leo, who admired her. Lyubov, however, naturally preferred the older boys. She indicated that Leo was too young to be interesting. In an impulsive gesture, intending to tease and perhaps frighten the girl, Leo gave her a little push. To his horror, Lyubov lost her balance on the balcony ledge and fell all the way to the ground. For a while afterward, she limped. Many years later she was to remind Leo of this incident.

A swarm of teachers came and went at Yasnaya. Fyodor Rössel was the first and best-liked of the tutors who lived with the children. He gave them an excellent knowledge of German, but not much more. When Papa, Grandmother, and the aunts thought it was time for Nicholas to prepare to enter a university, it was probably Grandmother who insisted that all the children be taken to Moscow to study with better professors. Count Nicholas agreed. He was often in Moscow anyway, visiting and gambling. He briskly made plans for the move. The time had come for the children to see that there was more to Russia than their quiet country home. Therefore, in January, 1837, the entire household left Yasnaya Polyana and moved to the city of Moscow. Leo Tolstoy was almost nine.

MOSCOW

The planning and packing for the family's move to Moscow went on for weeks. Countless boxes and trunks were loaded into a caravan of sledges and carts waiting in the snowy driveway. Praskovya, the old housekeeper, rattled the keys hanging on her belt and shouted to dozens of servants who struggled with the bundles. Champing and blowing in the frigid air, even the horses seemed eager to be off.

Leo wandered about in the confusion, stooping to hug his favorite dogs, feeling a strange homesickness already as he breathed their odor. Tearful peasants approached to say good-bye and to make the sign of the cross over him. The boy recalled the Christmas just past, the games and fun, the strange costumes and hilarity of the serfs. Yasnaya, my home, he thought, wiping his eyes on the sleeve of his coat. Why must they leave?

At the moment of departure the travelers gathered to pray in the drawing room. Following Russian tradition, all kept a silence of one minute together before leaving. Leo looked anxiously about the hushed group in heavy dark clothes. Here were Grandmother, his three brothers, his pretty sister Marya, the French governess, Aunt Alexandra lifting high a holy icon, Pashenka,

Fyodor Rössel, Aunt Tatyana holding Dunya's hand, and his handsome father, impatiently crossing himself, eager to be on his way. Thirty house servants were also to travel with the family.

At last the procession started. In the lead rumbled Grandmother's huge yellow cabriolet. The group stopped frequently, replenishing its water supply at streams along the snowy highway, changing to fresh horses, and making repairs when necessary. They spent three nights in smoky travelers' inns, the only available accommodations, which crawled with vermin. To keep the children contented on the journey of one hundred thirty miles, they were shifted from Papa's sledge to Grandmother's comfortable old carriage and then again to the coaches of the aunts. On the fourth day, just as the golden domes and cupolas of Moscow came shining into view, the caravan stopped again, and Leo was invited into Count Tolstoy's new sledge. It smelled deliciously of tobacco and leather upholstery. Seated beside his father as they entered the city, Leo could hardly contain his excitement. The count was also enjoying himself, gaily pointing out sights as the procession drove slowly through the noisy streets: the ancient church of St. Basil; the Kremlin's fortress wall of pink brick overlooking the river; the Borovitzkiye Gate, built before Columbus discovered America; the blazing domes crowning the Church of the Redeemer, largest church in all Russia. Despite his excitement, something troubled Leo. He knew his family was highly respected and widely acquainted, even here in Moscow; then why did the people on the streets take no notice of this long procession of coaches and carts? Everyone was treating them like strangers. Back in the country the peasants always bowed and took off their caps when the Tolstoys rode by. Here in Moscow, no one even spoke. Later, in his story *Boyhood*, Tolstoy recorded his sudden realization that a great world existed which was not even aware of his family. "Who lives in that house? Are there children, a father, mother, tutor? . . . What can they possibly be occupied with since they are not concerned with us?"

Soon the children were being introduced into the world of Moscow aristocracy and making friends. The lively city cousins who came visiting intrigued Leo. Now and then he forgot to be shy. At other times he would indulge in erratic behavior inspired by a deep desire to have everyone think him clever. Many years later, in *Childhood*, he noted the intoxicating experience of a first, childish love. The object of this "pure, strong, and good feeling" was Sonya Koloshin, a little beauty his age, ten. With her mother she attended a party given by the Tolstoys in the city. Dazzled and confused, Leo would never have guessed that her golden curls had been wound on bits of the *Moscow Gazette* for the entire day. His brain roared unusual commands. As he walked down the hall with Sonya past a dark closet, he found himself thinking strangely, "What happiness it would be if it were possible to spend one's whole life with her in this dark box room."

When the party had ended and the children were sent to bed, Leo remembered galloping through quadrilles, mazurkas, and waltzes, and conversing gaily in French and in Russian. The music of the orchestra ran through his mind, but Sonya with her bright cornflower eyes was the center of his thoughts. He punched Sergei, who was asleep in the next bed. Smiling in the dark, Leo told him that he'd fallen in love with Sonya Koloshin. Sergei opened one eye. Suddenly the younger brother asked, "Are you in love with her too?"

Sergei replied fiercely, "If I could I'd like to . . . kiss her on the fingers, the eyes, the lips, the nose, the feet. . . ." Leo thrust his head deep under the pillows. He had heard enough.

Nicholas would occasionally engage his youngest brother in deep discussions. At an early age Leo pondered life and death, happiness and pain. Only when one can bear suffering can one be happy, he decided. But he felt he already *knew* how to bear suffering. To prove it he heaved Grandfather's heavy dictionaries down from the shelf and held them rigidly at arm's length. His forehead grew damp. Red-faced, he muttered fiercely to himself that he could bear it for five minutes. At the end of that time he dropped the leather-bound volumes and flexed his aching arms, convinced that since he could endure pain, he could be happy.

In another of his turnabout moods, Leo would decide that happiness consisted of living only for the present. Then he would pamper himself with honeyed gingerbread and lounge for hours,

15

reading novels. That winter he started to write a story, "Grandfather's Tales," but after eighteen pages of heroes, battles, and bloodshed, he gave it up as a bore.

All the children respected their father, who seemed very much at home in the brilliant society of Moscow nobility. And as friends came calling, it was clear that Count Tolstoy had many admirers. Once they had settled in the city, the family saw him less. Sometimes in the schoolroom Leo would recite a favorite poem, Alexander Pushkin's "Napoleon," for him. Papa would listen intently, praising him and the other children. Then, pipe in hand, eyes sparkling, he would be gone again. Papa was always traveling. There were still lawsuits concerning the old debts of his father; he loved to hunt; and there were the several Tolstoy estates to look after. Then one day, while attending to business in the town of Tula, Count Tolstoy fell dead on the street.

The family in Moscow was thrown into a state of confusion and fear. Buttoning the children into hastily-stitched mourning clothes, the aunts wondered how they could manage the estates and household without the beloved Count. Leo moved aimlessly from room to room. He kept gazing through front windows, half expecting to see his father approaching. He felt empty. He recalled the tender way Papa had always helped Grandmother with her game of solitaire, their arrival in Moscow, and his strong hands which Leo had kissed so many times. The smell of Papa's Turkish tobacco wafted into his memory. Until now Leo had never realized how much he loved his father.

It was especially difficult for Grandmother to believe that Count Nicholas Tolstoy was dead. In a darkened room she spoke deliriously to her absent son. Grandmother seemed deranged, so pious Aunt Alexandra was appointed the children's guardian. But Grandmother recovered somewhat and became even more dictatorial. She took charge of dismissing the lax old tutor, Fyodor Rössel, complaining to Aunt Alexandra that the children were learning nothing. At her insistence a young French tutor was engaged. Prosper de St. Thomas was elegant and self-assured. He wore violet cologne. Rössel briefed his successor as he prepared to leave after his many years with the Tolstoy family. He wiped his blue eyes on a checkered handkerchief,

16

blew his large nose loudly, and in a broken voice advised the new teacher that the boys could best be taught by kindness.

Impatient St. Thomas sneered at such theatrics and made plans to be quite firm. He ignored Rössel and listened instead to a young student coach who reported, "Nicholas is both willing and able; Sergei is able but not willing; Dmitri is willing but not able; and Leo is neither."

Leo was not responding to his schoolwork. He missed the kind German tutor with his shabby clothes and comfortable ways, his simple dignity in the classroom. Mathematical drill bored Leo. He balked at memorizing historical dates, and stern St. Thomas' methods of physical punishment provoked him into shame and anger. The whip was rarely used, though frequently threatened. More often, when he had not prepared his lesson, Leo was forced into a dark closet and locked there for hours. The respect he learned for St. Thomas was tinged with hate.

In the gloom of the musty punishment closet, Leo's enraged imagination knew no bounds. He dreamed of sweet vengeance over his tormentor, the "foreigner," St. Thomas. These vivid fancies were later woven into the fiction of *Boyhood*.

> With my arm in a black sling I stroll along Tverskoy Boulevard. I am a general! . . . the well-known hero Nicholai. His Majesty comes up to me and says: ". . . I will do whatever you ask of me." I bow deferentially and say, leaning on my saber: "I am happy, Your Majesty, that I was able to shed blood for my country. . . . I have just one request: Allow me to destroy my enemy, the foreigner. . . ."

But the fantasy would shatter suddenly in the fear that St. Thomas himself might appear with a birch rod and find, not a defiant hero, but a cringing, humiliated crybaby. Sometimes the brooding boy blamed God for the injustice of his confinement: "I don't believe I forgot my prayers . . . , so why am I suffering?" The first seeds of religious doubt mingled with murderous imaginings. Neither the daydreams nor the discipline helped him to learn his lessons, and later Tolstoy called the shameful school-room punishment "the cause of the dreadful horror and repulsion toward every kind of violence" which he was to feel throughout his life.

Eleven months after Count Tolstoy's death, on a Sunday in May, 1838, another support of the family collapsed. That day a young friend had come to play with the Tolstoy brothers. He had hardly arrived when he called them together for a secret consultation. Triumphantly the visitor announced that at his high school a discovery had just been made—there is no God. The boys were electrified by such talk, but managed to conceal their lack of sophistication. They all agreed that such a theory was interesting, and probably true. Later the five indulged in the childish, forbidden game of burning paper in chamber pots. Just as they had achieved a crackling blaze and were gleefully feeding it, St. Thomas burst into the smoky room. "Your grandmother is dead!" The boys turned from their fire and stared at him in disbelief. Leo wept.

A glass-topped coffin arrived at the house, along with a solemn undertaker. Friends and relatives joined the self-conscious children, once again dressed in black mourning clothes. Leo could not help basking a bit in his deprivation. As he overheard visitors remark, "Complete orphans; their father only lately dead, and now the grandmother gone too," he enjoyed a stab of self-pity.

In July Aunt Tatyana headed back to the country with the three younger Tolstoys and Dunya. As her carriage wound its way up the familiar hill shaded by lime trees, the lonely old house gleamed ahead. After a few false yelps, the dogs remembered Leo and Dmitri and rolled in the sweet-smelling grass. But painful memories clouded the homecoming. Grandmother's aristocratic voice seemed to echo in the dining room. Papa's chair stood empty. When word spread that the Tolstoys had returned, the serfs came crowding in. Aunt Tatyana appeared, and the serfs in simple terms expressed their sorrow for the deaths of Count Tolstoy and his mother. Family and peasants shared tears.

During the rest of the summer, Aunt Tatyana taught the four young children French. For a short time Fyodor Rössel took his former stand in the schoolroom. St. Thomas had been left in Moscow, and the boys were delighted to have their kind German master back again. Leo was reading constantly. Russian legends appealed to him, as well as folk poems, the *Arabian Nights*, and the story of Joseph and his brothers from the Bible.

One afternoon he was returning from a walk around the grounds with his tutor. The two were talking in German when they noticed Kuzma, the groom, being dragged toward the barn by the steward. Leo asked where they were going. Rössel frowned. The steward replied tersely that they were going to the barn where Kuzma must be flogged. These words, and the sight of the miserable groom, bewildered the sensitive boy. That evening Leo told Tatyana about the incident. Auntie was horrified. "Why did you not stop him?" she asked. The gentle rebuke grieved Leo. He had had the power to prevent the beating, yet he had done nothing. A vivid picture of Kuzma being violently whipped rose repulsively in his imagination. He buried his face in his hands for shame.

Leo recalled a neighbor telling how he had once punished a serf by sending him to serve in the army. "I had a cook who took it into his head to eat meat during a [religious] fast and I sent him to serve as a soldier," the landowner asserted cheerfully. Why did that seem so wrong? the boy puzzled. It did not seem to worry the grown-ups.

In September, 1838, the family returned to Moscow for a special event. Nicholas I, Tsar of Russia and head of the Russian Orthodox Church, was laying the cornerstone for a new cathedral. In a suit with straps under the heels, Leo watched the ceremony with Auntie. As a military band stepped smartly down the street blaring martial music, Leo almost burst with pride. He wanted to put on a flashy uniform, to fight for his country, to die if necessary. Perhaps he would become a famous General Tolstoy!

The little family wintered in Moscow and returned to Yasnaya each summer. While the children grew, Aunt Alexandra shriveled to a mere shadow. One day she sent for them and prayed over each one. Then, sighing and making the sign of the cross, she asked to be taken to the convent at Optina-Pustyn for her last days. Surrounded by the chanting prayers of the nuns, she died there in 1841.

The children's security was shaken once again. In four years they had lost three loving guardians. Aunt Tatyana's serenity seemed shattered too. Several days after Alexandra's funeral, she called them in. They found her kneeling before her silver icon. Touching the cheek of each child, she said that she was being forced to send them to Kazan. Against their objections she explained that they must live with their father's sister, Pelagya Yushkov, their next of kin, and now by law their guardian. The children understood that Auntie Tatyana was only a distant cousin, but they felt that she had been in fact their mother. Why couldn't she move to Kazan also and live with them there? But this was impossible. Aunt Pelagya had never liked Tatyana. So Aunt Tatyana left to live with a sister far to the south.

Aunt Pelagya descended on Yasnaya Polyana with all the force, energy, and charm of a society dowager. She was not a brilliant woman; her social life was her overwhelming interest. But she was kind, and she felt that she could do as much for her brother's youngsters as Tatyana could. With a martyr's smile, Pelagya murmured quietly to one and all that she was willing to "sacrifice herself."

The move to Kazan was a monumental undertaking. Pelagya picked through the servants at Yasnaya Polyana. The most talented among them—serfs trained as cabinetmakers, tailors, upholsterers, locksmiths, cooks, and chambermaids—were sent by barge down the Oka River to the Volga and on to Kazan. Practically everything of value at the family home was packed up and barged away. When Pelagya set out to accomplish something, she was thorough. She knew how nobility should live, and she would raise these children according to her own standards. At her insistence, each boy was given a young serf to wait on him. Leo's servant, Alexis, stayed with him for the rest of his life.

Aunt Pelagya, Masha, Dunya, the four boys, and Prosper de St. Thomas made the trip to Kazan through the crisp November countryside in coaches. When the younger children mentioned how they missed Auntie Tatyana, Pelagya sniffed and shook her head impatiently. Long before the minarets of Kazan came in sight, Leo was wishing for the summer holiday, when he could go back to Yasnaya Polyana.

THE RESTLESS COUNT

Kazan was a port overlooking the Volga and Kazanka Rivers—a university town of about one hundred thousand people. The nobility among its inhabitants entertained each other constantly with costume balls, concerts, and theater parties. Aunt Pelagya considered it her duty to introduce her brother's children into this small but pretentious Kazan society. Her husband, Simon Yushkof, was a friendly, hideous-looking, large man, who wore a black mustache and grimaced constantly. Both guardians wanted the boys to become proper young noblemen, eligible for advantageous marriages and positions of importance, leading festive, idle lives. To be "proper," Leo remembered later in *Childhood*,

> consisted, first and foremost, in an excellent knowledge of French. . . . The second condition . . . was fingernails—long, manicured and clean; the third was an ability to bow, dance, and make conversation; the fourth, and a very important one, was . . . a constant expression of . . . refined superior boredom.

All these accomplishments would bring one up to a certain "proper" standard, called in French *"comme il faut"*—literally, "as it must be."

In his boyhood search for the man he would become, Leo wavered from one attitude to another, seeking a secure maturity, seeking a purpose—in truth, seeking himself. At times he made every effort to become a perfect *comme il faut* gentleman. In turn he would appear as philosopher, playboy, sometime scholar, gambler, or child of nature. When he attempted arrogant boldness, the budding aristocrats around him smirkingly called him "The Bear." When he exhibited awkward bashfulness, the young ladies of the ballrooms whispered behind their painted fans that Leo was "a boring partner." Furthermore, nature had not made him handsome. His nose was a large lump; his piercing gray eyes were small and quite unhappy with his face in the mirror. Aunt Pelagya saw that his clothes were stylish, but they never seemed to fit as well as Sergei's.

By 1843 Dmitri and Sergei had begun as first-year students at the University of Kazan. Nicholas had transferred here, too, from the University of Moscow. Sergei took joyously to the pleasant whirl of local society, but Dmitri was interested only in religion. He insisted that the whole family attend the Orthodox Church services. For himself he refused dancing, parties, and fine clothes. His best friend was a squint-eyed girl whom Aunt Pelagya had taken into the house out of pity. Acquaintances laughed at Dmitri, nicknaming him "Noah." One visitor could not understand his objection to dancing. "Noah, didn't you know that King David danced? Read it in the scriptures!" Leo, in his bumbling efforts to conform, also called his brother "Noah" and joined in teasing him.

Although Leo still prayed daily and kept the set fasts and holy days of the Orthodox Church, as most Russians did, by the age of sixteen he had almost stopped believing in "church" religion. The elaborate rituals, the pomp and ceremony, all seemed like tinsel attached to something far too immense and deep to be defined. He told himself that he could never stop believing in God. All his senses, and even his reason, told him that God

23

existed, always had and always would exist. However, he had begun to wonder if some of the things he had been taught about Him were true. When spring came, after the long white frozen months of winter, feelings of reverence overcame him. He would breathe the soft air joyously and prayerfully, and know that God was real. But, perhaps, he felt, he was not ready for Him yet.

The oral entrance examinations to the University of Kazan loomed ahead for Leo. Stifling his contempt for the tutor St. Thomas, he tried to apply himself to studying. In the spring of 1844 he presented himself for the tests. St. Thomas accompanied him, and was for once a comfort. Crisply turned out in new clothes for the occasion, Leo was extremely self-conscious. He took his place in the section of the lecture hall which was reserved for students of noble title. After a miserable wait, he heard his name called and went forward to face his tormentors, who were sitting on a platform at the end of the room. Their questions seemed to drift down from a great distance. He murmured back the vague wisps of answers that floated into his mind. Names and dates. I know nothing, the poor perspiring boy said to himself. Then came the questions in mathematics and statistics. Leo knew still less about these. He was praying desperately for a passing grade.

A new examiner stepped forward to question him in geography. Leo sighed with relief as he recognized a man who often visited his aunt's house. This was the gentleman who had urged Dmitri not to give up dancing for religion's sake, citing King David in the Bible. Smiling kindly at Leo, the trustee asked an easy question, "Please name the seaports in France." His face burning, Leo could not name one. With battered pride he left the crowded hall, the grim St. Thomas at his side. At sixteen Leo felt that he was not only a failure at these preliminary exams, but that his whole life was ruined. In two months he would try again. No Yasnaya Polyana vacation. He must study in steamy Kazan to be ready for the cursed reexamination.

After a miserable cramming season, he passed the fall exam. He had applied himself well. It was glorious to be accepted as a university student, to have his name printed in the directory, to wear a smart uniform with a sword and a cocked hat! Leo proudly chose the difficult College of Oriental Languages for his field.

But the new student did not feel a kinship with the mass of students. These poor sons of commoners with grimy fingernails and limited budgets were struggling to get the most out of their studies. Leo secretly longed to be admired by them, but for a long time he was too shy to get acquainted. Instead, he attended balls and dusk-to-dawn drinking parties with the ostentatious noblemen's sons, reeling home as the sun rose, missing the morning's classes. But Leo's merriment was frequently false.

At last he found a true friend in Mitya Dyakov, the tall, broad-shouldered son of a wealthy family. This friendship was to last for forty-five years. Shy, idealistic Dyakov was really Sergei's friend, but the younger brother was always hanging around, and Dyakov found Leo a partner for deep discussions. With Dyakov, Leo lost his brashness and timidity and became himself. Their talks would go on for hours. Ideas which had multiplied and stacked up in Leo's brain were unfolded, aired, and exchanged.

A new diary would also prove the comrade of a lifetime, filling many volumes. Among Leo's first entries was a list of "Rules" to live by. A straight and narrow path of goals, ambitions, duties and studies, enough to last for years, would be scheduled. These "Rules" were constantly amended and expanded—and almost always broken.

Soon he found it necessary to add a completely new Rule, "Keep away from women. . . ." This one was to be repeated countless times through the years, in one form or another. Women were beginning to glide frequently through his consciousness. He became uncomfortably aware that the chambermaids in his aunt's house were pretty girls and that Sergei was flirting with one of them. Leo discovered the anguish of vague temptations. He frequently found himself lingering on the landing outside the maids' room. Later he would characterize this time as the beginning of "a period of coarse dissoluteness." Furthermore, the pure, approved young ladies of the nobility were not responding wholeheartedly to his advances, though he fell in love two or three times: with Dyakov's lovely gray-eyed sister, Alexandra; with Zinaida Molostov, a school friend of his sister's; with a strange lady wearing pearls in a box seat at the theater.

On April 26, 1845, Leo's mail included a dismal notice from the Faculty of Oriental Studies. Because of "insufficient attendance in class and total failure in history," Leo was not allowed to take the year-end examinations. He was to be left a first-year student. Immediately, stormily, he blamed his history professor. He fumed, wept, and suffered, hiding himself indoors and upbraiding himself for idleness.

That spring Nicholas graduated from the University and left for Moscow to become a cadet in the Russian army. With Dmitri and Sergei, Leo crept home to Yasnaya Polyana, trying to forget his academic mortification. The old house caressed him gently. Memories always poured forth when he drifted back to this beloved spot. Again he seemed to smell the aroma of Papa's pipe, to hear his soft chuckle. There were the portraits of his ancestors looking down from the walls—the same faces, unimpressed with the progeny following them. The stair, the great hall, the drawing room—nothing had changed, but everything was somehow smaller, and he, Leo, had grown larger and older. He had changed, but, thank God, he was home at last. "Dear Lyovotchka!" Auntie Tatyana greeted him. He kissed her hand, conscious of her love, and his eyes filled with tears.

The next morning he was off to the river to swim and read under the birch trees, and to revel in bird songs, colorful wild flowers, and the forest fragrance. He carried a slim volume of Jean-Jacques Rousseau's *Confessions*. The summer was for reading. It was splendid to read what one liked, not what was assigned. And what Leo liked were the English novelists Laurence Sterne and Charles Dickens, and the French philosophers, especially Rousseau. Around his neck he wore a medallion with the image of Rousseau, whose ideas of equality were beginning to engage him. He visited the orchards and walked down to the shady ravine where the secret "green stick" of his childhood games was, presumably, still buried. The serfs bowed when they saw him, and he felt strange as he compared their state of servitude with the freedom advocated by Rousseau.

The summer was also for writing. He started three books:

26

Miscellany, consisting of poetry and philosophy; *What Is Needed for the Welfare of Russia?*; and *Observations on Property Management*. None was completed.

Leo had left his elegant *comme il faut* self behind in the Kazan ballrooms. Deciding here in the hills that fine clothes were pretentious, he sewed himself a shapeless canvas robe. Tied with a rope, it served for day and night—in fact, for an entire week. Simple slippers completed the costume. Aunt Tatyana was horrified when she caught sight of the flapping garment. But Auntie was patient with her favorite.

On his return to Kazan in the fall Leo stopped off to visit Nicholas, who was stationed with the 14th Artillery Brigade not far from Moscow. In a letter home Leo summed up his brotherly observation: "Poor fellow, he's having a miserable time in the camp. . . . You need only one glimpse . . . at first hand to lose all desire for a career in the army."

During their five years of living in Kazan the Tolstoy brothers had gone their separate ways. Serious and pious, Dmitri fasted, prayed, and eschewed society. Sergei dazzled his own rollicking social set and frequently went on wild sprees among the gypsies. Young Leo amused them both. In the fall of 1846, the three decided to live together in a rented cottage near the University. Now studying at the Faculty of Law, Leo found this year an interesting intellectual challenge. The lecturer in civil law assigned him a paper. Leo was to compare *Instruction*, a work by Catherine the Great, with *The Spirit of the Laws* by the French philosopher Charles de Montesquieu. Reading everything he could find on the subject, using all his thought, energy, and time to good purpose, something false seemed to loosen itself from his mind. He confided to his diary, "I am beginning to feel a passion for study growing within me. . . ." He felt he could learn more by himself than he could under any twenty dry professors. The boy suddenly seemed to find a man-sized purpose for himself. He wrote an excellent, mature treatise, then plunged into a variety of reading on every subject. But history was still a bore, and he could not bring himself to study it. The future author of *War and Peace* fretted, "History is nothing other than a collection of fables and useless trifles messed up with a mass of unnecessary dates and proper names."

On one of his examination papers his history teacher wrote, "Extremely lazy!" Leo boiled. Why should he take such rebukes when he was just beginning to love intellectual work?

Near the end of April in 1847, he applied for and received a release from the University. Without waiting for examinations, he packed his belongings and said good-bye to his brothers and the Yushkovs. A noisy farewell party was arranged by a large group of his friends, among them the admirable Dyakov. They all followed his coach as far as the Kazanka River, where they paused for final handshakes, shouted witticisms, and good-byes. From the cushions of his coach the dropout made elaborate plans to continue studying at Yasnaya. He listed among his intentions: "Study the entire law course, practical medicine . . . also French, Russian, German, English, Italian, and Latin, and agriculture . . . also history, geography, statistics. . . ." And the list continued.

What pleasure to turn up the winding drive and see Yasnaya, the home he thought so beautiful, appearing. He wrote immediately to aging Aunt Tatyana urging her to come home too. When she did and he had helped her move into her comfortable room, placing the icons on the wall and the jars of dried fruits on the dresser, they sat and talked happily in French. Sometimes Auntie called him Nicholas, thinking of his father, and blushed as she realized her mistake.

In July the oldest brother came on leave from the Russian army stationed far to the south in the mountainous Caucasus region. Nicholas was home for a special reason. Since Leo was eighteen and officially "of age," their mother's vast property, which had been held in trust, could now be divided. Dmitri and Sergei had been at home since their graduation. Marya also arrived, chattering about a certain handsome cousin, Valerian Tolstoy.

Under Russian law, daughters in a family were allowed only a tiny portion of an inheritance, the sons dividing the bulk of the estate. But the brothers decided that Marya should share

28

equally in their mother's property. She was allotted 2,440 acres of land and 150 serfs on the family's estate at Pirogovo, twenty-four miles from Yasnaya. Sergei took the horses, stud farm, and more lands on the same estate, where the hunting was excellent. Nicholas inherited another estate, Nikolskoye. Dmitri was given Sherbatchevka in Kursk. And Leo received Yasnaya Polyana, with its 4000 acres and 330 serfs.

It was Russian custom for the youngest son to inherit the family home, and Leo seemed to prefer it. Someone asked Sergei why Leo liked Yasnaya Polyana best. "It was considered the least profitable share of the entire estate," he replied. Embracing each other, the brothers scattered to appraise and admire their various lands, while Marya stayed at Yasnaya with Leo and Aunt Tatyana. In November she married her cousin, Valerian, and moved to Pokrovskoye.

Leo settled down to a season of contentment. He was reading ravenously, and faithfully keeping the diary in which he recorded not only his inmost thoughts and feelings, but also a list of his sins. This, he thought, would help him in his search for self-perfection. However, no matter how many lists of sins he made, the transgressions seemed to repeat themselves over and over, week after week.

He was proud to be a landowner. His novel *A Landowner's Morning* would outline his early experiences in this role. He had told Aunt Tatyana of the splendid plans he had made for his serfs. He wanted a school for the children, housing, more nourishing food, and better sanitary conditions for all. It was known that half of the serfs spent every kopek for drink. He felt he must help them. Tatyana wondered how long this settled-down Leo would last.

For the next eighteen months he made a sustained effort to deal generously with the serfs. But whatever he offered them was met with suspicion. Their attitudes were based on a lack of trust centuries old. At last he had the school started. A sprinkling of dingy, nervous children trooped daily to the big house for lessons. Leo himself helped with the teaching. Later it became clear that the peasants did not want their children to attend classes and would keep them away if they could. In addition to the serfs' mistrust, there was also the practical desire to keep the children home to help with farming and housework.

Though Leo presented the serfs with fine new plows of sharp iron, he would find them still pushing the ancient wooden *sokha* of their forefathers, an instrument which barely scratched the surface dust. They looked at him skeptically, and secretly lost their respect for a master who wanted to work with them. When he built more convenient houses to replace their mud isbas, he found them smiling, bowing politely, and stubbornly refusing to move in.

The problems the serfs brought for Leo to settle were usually insoluble. He would often find serfs gathered on the front steps of his mansion. One day a woman in bloody rags screamed that her father-in-law had tried to kill her. Before Leo could answer, the gardener brought a drunken relative for him to reprimand. Two brothers were arguing over a section of land, glowering at each other and at him. Leo wanted to offer them understanding, wise words, and perfect solutions, but his youth and inexperience left him wretchedly empty of answers. The peasants showed him dutiful deference, but they could not follow his lead to a more prosperous and comfortable life. Why did he not simply set them free? The idea did not occur to him until years later.

Finally he let the serfs go their own ways. The school was dropped. Its only serious problem had been absenteeism. The plans for housing improvements were curtailed. The serfs resumed their ancient, inefficient agricultural methods. They reverted to the traditional, odorous cabbage soup, dark bread, and buckwheat porridge. They returned to excessive drinking. The peasants were relieved and comfortable again; the young Count felt a complete sense of frustration.

In October, 1848, Tolstoy headed for the city. He was to spend three frivolous winters in Moscow and St. Petersburg, making the rounds of pompous high society, alternately enjoying and being bored by it, trying to forget his failure to improve the lives of his serfs.

In 1849, with two friends, he traveled on to St. Petersburg, the Capital of All the Russias, where the Tsar had his palace. Leo was charmed by the marble buildings, the air of industry, the

LEO TOLSTOY AROUND
AGE 20

STEPHEN GAMMELL

social circles. "I intend to remain here forever," he wrote to Sergei. With a little study he passed some of the law exams at the St. Petersburg University and considered taking a degree. Unfortunately, the green-covered card tables beckoned him away from the study desk, and Leo fell prey to the gambling virus. This was far from unusual. Many sons of wealthy families lost money at cards. To the list of the "Rules" in his diary, Leo now added "Rules for Card-Playing." He was positive he could win by his intellect. Instead, he lost his way seriously into debt.

Sergei had warned him against gambling. "With your scorn for money," Sergei had written, revealing an instinct based on experience, "you may well lose a large amount."

Leo replied with a plea that his brother sell his woodlot and several horses, for he needed money urgently. Then followed an even more desperate letter marked "Do not show this letter to Auntie. . . ."

> I think you are already saying I am a most frivo-
> lous fellow! . . . I went to St. Petersburg without
> any reason; there I have done nothing necessary,
> only spent a heap of money and run up debts!
> . . . You can't believe how it torments me. . . .
> Be so kind as to . . . get me out of this false and
> odious position. . . .

Sergei rescued his brother by selling one of Leo's farms. Along with the land, twenty-two serfs were sold. Serfs were often sold with the soil this way. It was the custom of the day. Oblivious of these souls and bored with the capital, Leo returned to Yasnaya and took a part-time job at nearby Tula with the Assembly of Nobles. Gypsy musicians lived nearby. Like Sergei, he went visiting among the dark-eyed girls and returned late at night, smelling of champagne and humming folk tunes. The next day he would make promises to his diary to reform. That very night might find him losing 4,000 rubles to a card-playing neighbor. Flirting with peasant women, he was frequently filled with pity for them and disgust for himself. He decided that country life held as many temptations as the city and left for Moscow. Again he tended his ego in fashionable drawing rooms, courted a princess or two, and admitted to his diary, "I am living a completely brutish life. . . ." In debt from losing at billiards and cards, he seriously considered applying for the job of postmaster on the mail run from Moscow to Tula. But on January 18, 1851, he jotted down a more interesting resolve: "To write the history of my childhood." This novel, *Childhood*, would make him famous several years later. From the landowner, the gambler, and the playboy, might an author be emerging?

Not yet. He put down his pen and pulled up again to the card tables, falling deeper into debt as each hand was dealt. It appeared that the young man, Leo, would never find the great man, Tolstoy.

THE CAUCASUS

As spring approached in 1851, Tolstoy came home to Yasnaya Polyana, tired of the pretense of fashion and depressed by his losses at cards. He was twenty-two. He had written his Aunt, "One regrets the past, the wasted time, one repents of one's weakness and the future lies ahead like a shining light." In Moscow and St. Petersburg he had achieved social acceptance among fellow aristocrats and beautiful women, but it all seemed a handful of ashes. He longed for a way of perfecting his spirit, along with an opportunity to distinguish himself, a chance for glory.

Lenten fasting gave way to Easter feasting when Nicholas arrived on leave from several years' military duty in the Caucasus. He was accompanied by their sister, Marya, a proud mother, with her husband Valerian, and their small son. The brothers and sister were delighted to be together again, but for Leo it was best of all to be with the mature, respected officer, Nicholas. Leo was flattered by the prospect of accompanying his dignified brother when he returned to duty. The Caucasus was a world of rugged mountain terrain, male glory, and heroic daring. What better place for a young man bored with society and already finding his country home a little bit dull? Although he had been at Yasnaya only a few weeks, Leo could hardly wait to leave with Nicholas. Perhaps he too would find glory in a military career. Valerian agreed to manage the estate in his absence, paying Leo's debts with the income from crops and forests at Yasnaya Polyana.

Since Nicholas had a month of his military furlough left, the brothers decided to head north to Moscow for some society before leaving for the wilds. In Moscow Leo subscribed to a lending library, assuring himself plenty of reading for the mountains. Then going even farther out of their way, they visited Kazan. In front of Aunt Pelagya's house Leo climbed a tree for old times' sake. The brothers roamed the halls of the University of Kazan, and were entertained by old friends. Despite his determination to turn his back on society, Leo enjoyed it immensely and thought he cut a rather fine figure.

One day Leo pointed out a man on the streets. "It's obvious that man is a scoundrel," he said to Nicholas.

"Why?" his brother inquired.

"Because he is without gloves."

"But why is he a scoundrel if he doesn't wear gloves?" Nicholas looked at Leo with a slow smile. The younger man was embarrassed, realizing how immature his judgment must seem.

Leo took a walk in an archbishop's garden with Zinaida Molostov, a friend from long ago. She cast warm glances at her hesitant escort, but there was no time for a declaration of love. Nicholas was impatient to get on his way.

As Leo climbed aboard the coach, his brother complained that he must have changed his shirt a dozen times in Kazan. Leo replied slyly that Nicholas was the man he most admired, except for his dirtiness.

Soon their entire carriage, including Leo's dog Boulka and the baggage, was flatboating down the icy Volga River, moving with current, oars, and sails. It was an unforgettable experience for Leo: the gray river, the boatmen's songs, the white sails; the early morning sun sweeping away the fog as they floated past the green and thawing countryside. A month later they came to the unbelievable mass of snowy mountains near the sea, the Caucasus.

Located about nine hundred miles southeast of Moscow, between the Black and Caspian Seas, the mountain peaks of the Caucasus, higher than the Alps, separate Europe from Asia Minor. Tsar Alexander I had annexed the area in 1801, and for fifty years, bitter fighting had existed between the savage Moslem mountain people, the Circassians, and their enemies, the Russian frontiersmen called Cossacks. The Cossacks were bolstered by the Tsar's troops—among them Artillery Lieutenant Nicholas Tolstoy—and a string of forts. Most dreaded of the Circassian tribes were the Chechenians ("Cherkes"), who boasted two brutal, daring chieftains, Shamil and Hadji Murad. Although the number of warriors in both armies was small, raids and expeditions often resulted in civilian murders, ruined countryside, stolen livestock, and hardship for the general population. There were no holds barred in this grimy little war which seemed to have no end.

As Leo traveled beside his brother, he thought that this place was unlike any he had seen. The majestic peaks in the distance actually moved him to prayer. He breathed the fragrance of white acacia blossoms. Rushing streams from high up gave off a steamy vapor, and handsome women in colorful eastern costume washed clothes in the natural hot springs. The native girls seemed frank and free compared to the careful, coquettish socialites Leo had known in Moscow. The people, dignified and very proud, lived in reed-thatched huts.

A battery of Russian soldiers was stationed in a little village near Fort Stary Yurt. Leo won the confidence of these uneducated men and made friends among the natives; his understanding of the common people and the poor was growing. In such simple people he felt he saw more natural and generous motives than he had known in the many opportunists of high society.

With the officers, on the other hand, Leo found himself shy and ill at ease. At first they thought him standoffish, a snob. They called him "Count" and complained among themselves that he was just a civilian along for the ride. They had their duty, a job to do, a land to conquer. The commander, Lt. Colonel Alexeyev, was a pious, admirable man with blond sideburns. One of his ears had been bitten off by a horse, but he carried his jaunty little frame with true military bearing. He greeted Leo cordially and invited him to dinner. Drinking was forbidden at the commander's table, but the officers slaked their thirst later in their tents, and the gambling often went on all night long. Against his best intentions Leo was soon playing cards every night after supper. Scolding himself bitterly for this practice, he nonetheless relaxed in the games and began to enjoy the officers —boyish Buyemsky; the simple old captain, Khilkovsky; coarse Lt. Knorring, whom Leo privately called "Hammerhead"; easy, obliging Groman; unlucky Stansulevitch; belligerent Ensign Yanovitch; and Zuyev, a pretentious chatterer who sprinkled his speech with foreign words.

One night after supper Leo noticed among the gamblers a friend of his, a native named Sado who worked with the Russians. Sado was bright, but he could not add figures. Now he groaned over his gambling losses. It was obvious that he was being cheated. Leo looked around the table at each guilty face: embarrassed Khilkovsky; flushed Buyemsky; Knorring, who coughed and would not meet his eye. Taking Sado in tow, Leo began to watch the scorekeeping to prevent the officers from further swindling. Sado swaggered with pleasure. He told Leo that they would be *kunaks*, friends for life. Presenting his champion with a silver bridle and a sword, he assured Leo that anything he owned he would share with his *kunak*. Sado's father was a wealthy native, but he kept his money buried in an old pot and shared none of it with his son. The handsome youth, who lived by daring and stealing, had at times as much as a thousand rubles; at other times, nothing. He was idolized by the village girls. Leo cast about for some sort of reciprocation and finally gave Sado a gun and a silver watch, which actually belonged to Nicholas.

Another of Leo's Cossack friends was Epishka, whose livelihood was hunting and horse thievery. Red-faced, wearing a fur hat and a long scraggly white beard, Epishka voiced his opinions boisterously, honestly, and often. He smelled of gunpowder, animal hides, and drink. Leo saw him as a kind of "noble savage" like those natural men idealized by Rousseau. Together the two men hunted hare, foxes, teal, snipe, pheasant, and other game. Although Epishka must have been nearly eighty, he still admired the lovely barefooted village girls as they helped with the grape harvest or gathered watermelons and sunflowers. The Count amused him, and Leo was fascinated by this free, illiterate giant who seemed the complete master of his environment.

There were two kinds of girls in this remote village. There was the kind he would like to scrub before he touched, and then there was Maryanka. Maryanka was the proudest of the Cossack girls. To lonely Leo Tolstoy, she seemed to express all of nature's loveliness. Each day, dressed in a simple pink smock, she strode past his hut on the way to work in her father's fields. In spite of his dissatisfactions here, Leo dreamed of marrying Maryanka, becoming a Cossack, and living the rest of his life in these exquisite wilds. When he achieved success with women, Leo groveled in shame; when he or they remained aloof, he was miserable.

And the old passion for gambling was plunging him into debt again. How could he handle this craving for nightly card games? He had been toying with the idea of writing a short novel based on his childhood. To immerse himself in some sort of work might save him from the lure of the gaming tables. He must learn to write. And he needed money; why not earn some? Writing and publishing novels was not a bad way to make a living. He decided to devote part of each day to his novel, part to study, part to enjoyment, with a little time left for his diary.

Early that summer the Russian army moved forward. Gun carriages and cannons were pulled over the mountains. Eager to see some military action, Leo requested permission to go along as a volunteer. He loved the songs of the soldiers, the clank of the weapons, and the views from the snow-covered heights. Even so, two small, cold fears lodged in his mind. There was the fear that he might die under fire or be maimed. Even worse, he thought, "What I am afraid of is not being able to bear pain and death with dignity."

The Russians destroyed a deserted village. Then, as the little army was returning to Fort Stary Yurt, enemy hill tribes—the Cherkes—attacked. Muskets cracked. With a sense of unreality amid the confusion and firing, Leo saw several soldiers clutch their bodies and slump forward. One moaned awhile, then was still. Fear passed through the young Tolstoy. His throat was parched and his hands shook, but he managed to keep his composure. The battery quickly returned fire, and the attackers departed at last. When the battleground was quiet, three Russian soldiers lay dead and thirty-six more were wounded. Soon after this, Leo was surprised to hear General Baryatinsky praising him for his calm bearing under fire. The general advised him to apply for a commission. Visions of greatness swam before Leo's eyes. Perhaps he would be awarded the Cross of St. George for gallantry. The limp, crumpled bodies being lifted onto stretchers faded from his thoughts.

In his notebook he nursed expanding ambitions: to obtain a commission, to achieve the Cross of St. George, to become a successful writer, to perfect himself morally, and even to benefit mankind. With egotistical awe he secretly confessed, "There is something in me which compels me to believe that I was not born to be like everybody else."

In November he set out for the warm cosmopolitan town of Tiflis to take the examination for induction into the army. He found that he needed certain papers which must be sent from officials at Tula in his home province. Waiting in Tiflis for their arrival, he rented quarters in a garden suburb overlooking the Kura River.

He now determined to continue his short novel. It was taking shape as a fictional autobiography of his early years. Memories flooded over him as he thought of home and those days. He scribbled a quick letter to Aunt Tatyana:

> Do you remember, dear Aunt, the advice you once gave me—to write novels? Well, I am following your advice. . . . I do not know if what I am writing will ever be published, but it is work that amuses me and in which I have persevered too long to abandon it.

What was leading him to complete at last this work he had planned for an entire year? Money. He realized, to his sorrow, that the desire for money motivates much in life, although it is often concealed. He had fallen into debt again last fall when he had lost five hundred rubles in a card game with Lt. Knorring. Knorring had agreed to accept notes for delayed payment, and to wait until January; but January was approaching rapidly. Leo might be reported to Colonel Alexeyev or even to General Baryatinsky. His chances for glory would certainly be lost. Writing rather desperately now, he wondered how much money a first novel would bring. Just a few days remained until the debt of honor was due. That night he prayed, "Lord, help me!"

The next day he opened a letter from Stary Yurt. Nicholas had great news for him:

> Sado came to see me. He has won your notes-of-hand from Knorring and has brought them to me. He was so pleased to have won them, and asked me so often, "What do you think? Will your brother be glad that I have done this?" that I have grown very fond of him. That man is really attached to you.

The *kunak*, disobeying Leo's advice against gambling, had played with Lt. Knorring and won back the fat notes bearing Tolstoy's signature. With typical careless gallantry, Sado had tossed the papers to Nicholas, asking him to send them on to Leo as a gift. Now Leo emptied the contents of Nicholas' envelope across his desk. He was amazed. He felt he could hold up his head again. He wrote immediately to Aunt Tatyana, telling her the entire story, the prayer for deliverance, its miraculous answer, and his present relief:

> Is it not astonishing to see one's petitions granted like this the very next day? That is to say, there is nothing so wonderful as the divine goodness to one who merits it so little as I. And is not the trait of Sado's devotion admirable? . . . Please have a six-barreled pistol bought in Tula and sent

to me, and also a music box if that does not cost too much. These are things which will give him much pleasure.

Finally Leo received a provisional assignment with Nicholas' battery in the 20th Artillery Brigade. Buttoned into a brand-new uniform, he twirled his mustache and wrote Sergei that he was now ready to destroy those "turbulent Asiatics." He fell into the routine with gusto. There were expeditions, skirmishes, drills, and marches. He thanked God for leading him to such a life. He learned to present a cool front under fire, and this behavior in battle did not go unnoticed by his superior officers. Recommended twice for the Cross of St. George, which he so badly wanted, he found to his painful disappointment that it could not be awarded him because the papers from Tula still had not come.

When the spring campaigns were over, Leo got a health leave to go to a nearby spa. He was suffering from toothache, rheumatism, and dysentery. The resort town, Pyatigorsk, became very gay in the summer when visitors arrived to take the waters and enjoy the gathered society. For four months Leo followed doctor's orders; he drank the warm water, which smelled of minerals, and bathed in it every day until his skin was lobster red. He clowned and conversed and relaxed from war. It was good to leave tents, guns, and men for a while, to rest here where pretty girls wore pastel dresses and orchestras were playing in the fresh air, while on the distant mountains snow shone white as sugar.

At Pyatigorsk, Leo completed his first novel, *Childhood*. When he had begun it, he had had no idea that so much work would be involved. For a year now he had outlined and planned, written and rewritten at Tiflis, at Stary Yurt, and even with his troops on expedition. Intelligent copyists were difficult to find. Vanyushka, a serf, was helping him copy it, but he became sick, and Leo stopped work to nurse him. On July 3, 1852, he completed the final copy of the novel and sent it to a famous St. Petersburg magazine, *Contemporary*. A humble letter accompanied Leo's story. He had no idea whether the well-known editor, Nekrasov, would publish his novel, or, if he did, how much money it might bring. Signing only his first two initials, L. N., he asked the editors not to make his name public.

Two months later, on the day after his twenty-fourth birthday, a letter came from Nekrasov:

> I have read your manuscript. It is so far interesting and I will print it. It seems to me . . . that the author is a man of talent.

When Leo saw those words, he felt he had found his life's work. He would be successful. Fame and riches, glory and a perfect life would be his. But when, he wondered, would *Contemporary* send him the money for his novel? Another letter from the editor settled this problem. Nekrasov said that it was not customary to pay a beginning writer for his first published work. He promised that in the future Tolstoy would receive the top price: fifty rubles for every sixteen printed pages. The beginner stopped momentarily. Then, in spite of the disappointment, he felt a surge of joy. His pleasure was doubled when *Contemporary* arrived in October containing his work in print.

The novel was an immediate success. Leo had transformed his memories into bright, original fiction. The style was a copy of no one else's and the story was charmingly realistic.

Several weeks later the new author was spending the night in a forest cabin with some fellow officers after a hunting trip. In a little magazine he came across a review praising *Childhood* and congratulating its author, L. N. He lay across his bunk and silently exulted, keeping this secret to himself. It satisfied him, strangely, that not one of his hunting companions realized how famous he was.

His sister, Marya, had not known of Leo's writing. One day a neighbor, the famous author Ivan Turgenev, brought her a copy of *Childhood*. Turgenev had just completed an important work called *A Sportman's Sketches*. The tall, elegant gentleman settled himself familiarly in an armchair in his neighbor's parlor and began to read bits of *Childhood*. Marya listened politely, then with more interest as Turgenev seemed to be reading stories from *her* childhood—-the family's move to Moscow; the description of

Grandmother; blue-eyed Sonya Koloshin whom Leo and Sergei had both loved; the children acting out scenes from *The Swiss Family Robinson*; the old German tutor and the jaunty young French one. Turgenev's smooth voice read on, but Marya was wondering, "Who could have written it? Who could know all the little intimate details of our life?" They decided that Nicholas must be the unknown author; but of course, the truth was soon discovered. Turgenev wrote to Nekrasov applauding the story. Indeed, praise flowed from all sides to author and to editor.

Meanwhile, Leo shuttled from battlefield to writing table, from pen to gun. He was finding authorship more and more to his liking, his military duties less interesting and often distasteful. Soon a story called "The Raid," drawn from his life in the army, was on its way to *Contemporary*. In this frank sketch, as in later works, the realism and violence of the soldiers' experiences were exposed. But before the story reached the publisher, military censors cut away the parts of the work in which the brutalities of war were most clearly revealed. The government censors' scissors seemed to draw blood as they snipped from "The Raid" Tolstoy's sincere efforts. For the first time in his life he felt gagged.

An incident in June, 1853, turned up years later in Tolstoy's favorite story, "A Prisoner in the Caucasus." One warm day he and his friend Sado were almost captured by the Chechenians as they hurried toward Fort Grosnaya on horseback. The tribesmen could easily have shot them, but probably planned to take them prisoner and torture them. The two were about to be overtaken when the gates of the fort came into sight, and they went flying in.

But such excitement was rare. For the most part military life was a matter of boredom. "This damned army detachment," he scrawled in the faithful notebook. Tolstoy disliked the inane conversation of the officers and the colonel's eternal enthusiasm for discipline. Only writing made Leo's life interesting. He finished the first draft of *Boyhood*, a sequel to *Childhood*, in July. *Youth*, another sequel, was under way; so was "Memoirs of a Billiard-Marker."

He felt so good when he was exerting himself. Picking up pen and notebook one day, he realized that his hand actually trembled with excitement. He jotted some "Rules for Writing" into his diary:

> When rereading and revising do not think about what should be added (no matter how admirable the thoughts that come to mind) . . . but about how much can be taken away without distorting the overall meaning. . . . The most interesting books are those in which the author pretends to hide his personal opinion and yet remains faithful to it.

Far more frequently the diary contained thoughts about God and about good and evil, and confessions of conduct with native girls that Tolstoy felt to be humiliating:

> My life is extremely disorderly so that I do not recognize myself, and I am ashamed to live like this. . . . Sensuality gives me not a moment's peace. . . . The sight of any woman's naked foot makes me think her beautiful. . . . Girls have led me astray. . . . I have done much evil. . . .

He longed for home and family, and knew now that a military career was not for him. He was becoming very sensitive to the injustice of the border war. Sometimes he wondered, "Am I doing right?"

> Because of girls whom I do not have, and the cross [of St. George] which I shall not get, I live here, wasting the best years of my life. It is stupid.

As he sent in his resignation to the army, war clouds of a serious nature were gathering in another corner of Russia. By midsummer, Russian troops had entered the Danube principalities of Moldavia and Walachia. England and France were arming. In such troubled times, the army refused to release

44

Cadet Tolstoy. Therefore he decided to become a real warrior. He made every effort to obtain a commission and to get himself transferred to the war zone near the Black Sea.

Here in the grimy Caucasian war, rumors were flying that Shamil was preparing 40,000 Tartars for an attack. Meanwhile, on October 20, 1853, Tsar Nicholas I declared war on Turkey, and the Danubian struggle between world powers was on. Tolstoy's transfer orders arrived at last on January 12, 1854, along with the assurance of a commission. He was trading the Caucasus for Rumania, and suddenly he felt a lump in his throat. He got leave so that he could touch base once more at Yasnaya Polyana. As he looked into his friends' faces, saying good-bye, he felt he was almost leaving a home here too. His officer-companions celebrated his promotion. The Cossacks cheered him. Epishka and Sado came to the road to say farewell. In the Caucasus he had found neither glory nor self-perfection, but places and people he would never forget, along with a profession: writing.

WAR IN THE CRIMEA

A violent snowstorm preceded Leo to Yasnaya. Cold white drifts reached above the double windows on one side of the old house, but the warmth of home was within. Aunt Tatyana, tiny and shriveled, came forward. Leo kissed her hands, eager to share his experiences in the Caucasus and the story of his successful writing venture. He found all three brothers waiting to hail him. Backslapping greetings and manly Russian embraces were exchanged. Then came an excellent meal and hours of talk, as the drawing room darkened and thickened with smoke, opinions, and the loud male chatter of swapped experiences. The old clock on the landing chimed one, then two, and was ignored. Unwilling to end their conversation, the happy brothers bedded down together on the drawing-room floor, where they slept at last.

Determined to make the most of Leo's leave before sending him off to conquer the Turks, the young men soon galloped to Moscow to see friends and enjoy the city happenings. Here the warrior outfitted himself in fine military fashion, admiring his mirror image with its muttonchop whiskers and dress uniform. Glaring into a large black box camera (and reeking of hair oil), the brothers had a group picture made. Then as the hours of furlough ran out, they circled by Marya's home at Pokrovskoye, where Aunt Pelagya was visiting. The final stop was Dmitri's estate, Sherbatchevka. Auntie Tatyana met them again to take one last look at Leo, her favorite. All cried, and Leo felt he had never been so surrounded by love. Pleased with himself, he waved once more to his family and stepped into the waiting sledge.

Fourteen hundred bone-wearying miles lay ahead of him. When the snow turned to mud, the comfortable sledge had to be exchanged for a jarring cart with no springs. He arrived, exhausted, on March 12, 1854, at Bucharest, the first European city he had ever seen. The streets of the crowded town were narrow and crooked, but hummed with undeniable gaiety. The ensign met a few young noblemen, looked in on a French theater and an Italian opera, and finally dropped his worried aunt a quick note:

> I have a fit of conscience when I think that you believe me exposed to every danger, while I've still not smelt Turkish powder and live here tranquilly at Bucharest, promenading about, occupied with music, and eating ice cream.

The war was beginning around the Black Sea, Russia's southern boundary. This large body of warm water was highly important to Russian shipping because its ports were open in winter. The narrow straits leading from the Black Sea to the Mediterranean were Russia's winter gateway to the world. Over these straits, the Dardenelles and the Bosporus, Turkey and its failing Ottoman Empire stood a weak guard. Tsar Nicholas I, ignoring his own people's domestic problems, had sent armies into the Black Sea area in the summer of 1853 to show Turkey that he could control this strategic shipping outlet.

In fact, there were many causes for this needless war, some politically complicated, some ridiculous. A few of the complex reasons were rooted in the proud personalities of rulers. The Tsar hoped to raise himself in Russian popularity by proving his power over the Turks. Queen Victoria and England were maneuvering to begin the Suez Canal nearby and wanted no interference from Russia. Napoleon III of France, nephew of Napoleon Bonaparte, felt that the blue-blooded Tsar had acted badly toward him. Nor could he forget how the French had been outwitted by the Russians in 1812. France and England thus became allies for the first time in two hundred years. Another monarch, the Austrian emperor, was settled on a rather shaky throne. Along with France and England, Austria vastly overrated the might of the Russian army. All these powers nervously watched together as Russian General Gorchakov mobilized his little army.

When Tolstoy had reached Bucharest, he had reported to the palace headquarters of Commanding General Prince Michael Gorchakov. The prince wore a cap on the back of his head, clasped his hands behind his back, and spoke quickly, decisively, not unlike a tom turkey. Leo was flattered and pleased to be warmly greeted by this commander, who was also a distant relative. Soon Ensign Tolstoy was made a courier, taking messages from one general's office to another. He wrote up military reports, and in his spare time finished *Boyhood*, sending it to *Contemporary* to follow the successful *Childhood*.

In May of 1854 Gorchakov's troops were ordered to besiege Silistra, a town sixty miles southeast of Bucharest, on Turkish soil. The invading army settled quickly into magnificent surroundings on high ground among the regal gardens of the border city's governor. From his perch among the cannon Leo could look down on the town and several small forts located in the islands of the Danube. Parts of the bank were held by the Turks, parts by the Russians. The fascinated young officer felt his blood warm as he looked below. Could those black moving specks be soldiers? A spyglass proved that the specks in the panorama below were indeed uniformed men. They looked like the miniature lead army which had battled long ago on the rug at Yasnaya Polyana. A shattering cannonade jolted him back to reality.

Back and forth the new courier was sent. To the trenches with orders, dodging bullets. To the commanders, reporting his observations. Prince Gorchakov seemed so splendid and poised under fire. He simply did not recognize danger for himself; but he was always concerned for his men. The final attack and capture of Silistra and its surroundings was planned for June 9 at three A.M. Every man, every gun was in readiness. General Gorchakov had overlooked nothing. Leo recalled his vivid memory of that day in a letter to Tatyana and Nicholas:

> I am going to tell you of my recollections of Silistra. . . . One heard the booming of cannon and musket-shots unceasingly day and night, and with a spyglass could . . . see people killing one another. . . .
>
> We were all there, and as usual on the eve of the battle we all pretended not to think of the morrow. . . . As you know . . . fear is a most disagreeable feeling. Toward morning, the nearer the moment came the more the feeling diminished, and toward three o'clock when we were all expecting to see a shower of rockets let off which was the signal for the attack, I was . . . well inclined for it. . . . And there! Just an hour before the time . . . orders to raise the siege of Silistra! . . . This news was received by all, soldiers, officers, and generals, as a real misfortune. . . .

But word reached the field marshal that Austria had amassed a large army on the Turkish border. The allies pressured Russia into leaving Turkish territory. So the planned Russian siege of Silistra was revoked at the last moment. None of this was explained to officers or men.

The war should have ended at that point, but did not. By July, France and England had grown tired of waiting for a possible attack from Russia. They decided to invade the Crimea, a peninsula jutting deeply into the Black Sea and narrowly joined to mainland Russia. It would not take long, allied commanders reasoned, to conquer this vulnerable target, which had been for years the summer home of the tsars. On August 26 the largest army ever sent overseas set out—57,000 combined French and Englishmen, eager to take over the fight against the Russians.

The Turks were willing to let them. Continuing the war was actually a mistake. Russia had backed away from foreign soil and was no longer a threat. Even so, as Tolstoy noted, when armies are poised for battle, it is difficult to restrain them.

Tolstoy spent the summer in Bucharest, drilling with his men, writing, enjoying cards and society. After talking with a friend one night about Russian serfdom, he remarked lightly to his diary, "It is true that slavery is an evil thing, but ours is a very benevolent evil." Then, along with his volumes of Goethe and Schiller, he read a German translation of the American anti-slavery novel, *Uncle Tom's Cabin*, which was banned at the time in Russia. Impressed by the content of this work, he reexamined his thoughts about slavery; a year later he would record this new idea: "I must accumulate money, (1) to pay my debts, (2) to . . . make it possible to liberate my serfs."

Meanwhile, lofty in his longing to serve others, Tolstoy the altruist suffered a disaster at the card table. He lost his estate—or part of it. The central structure of the house at Yasnaya, in which he had been born, was taken down, beam and sill, and sold to a neighbor for five thousand rubles to pay his gambling debts. Of Grandfather Volkonsky's showplace only two large wings remained, with a terrace in between. Nicholas kindly wrote to say that the place didn't look bad at all. Tolstoy felt too guilty to even confess the loss in his diary, but he repeatedly deplored his "idleness, irritability, and lack of character."

As he searched the shortcomings in himself, Tolstoy was alert to the admirable qualities of the men around him. Poorly equipped, ill-trained, ill-clad, ill-fed, and often ill-led, the Russian soldiers nonetheless displayed a courage, a spirit, and a will far beyond those of their more numerous counterparts in the well-provisioned allies. Tolstoy decided that something should be done for the morale of these seldom-celebrated Russian heroes. In a letter to Sergei he outlined a plan for a military magazine he wanted to publish on their behalf:

> It would be a cheap magazine (three rubles a year) and a popular one, that soldiers may read it. . . . We should publish descriptions of battles—

not such dull and not such inaccurate ones as are
given in other magazines—courageous exploits,
biographies, and obituary notices of worthy . . .
obscure men; military stories, soldiers' songs. . . .

When his battery was moved to Kishinev, Tolstoy approached
a friend with the idea for the soldiers' magazine. The officer,
Komstadius, shared his literary interests. He was enthusiastic
about the plan. The two set to work. Tolstoy began to write
realistic stories and articles about military life. Why not let
everyone know what true war was like? Why not jolt the high
command into improving the lot of the little man? He described
how recruits were flogged to teach them to obey. He told of the
courageous, dying Russian soldier of the battlefield in "How
Russian Soldiers Die." He felt he must present the truth. Prince
Gorchakov encouraged the bold editors and sent their sample
magazine, *The Military Gazette,* to the Minister of War for his
approval. The grand project was immediately crushed. The government's aim was for more discipline among the troops, not
less. *The Military Gazette* might throw a harsh light on the war
and perhaps render it unpopular just when the Tsar most needed
public support. Rulers and military brass thought it necessary for
the people to applaud the fiercest carnage as a "glorious, heroic"
conflict.

Reports from the front were far from glorious. French and
English forces had landed in the Crimea in September and had
defeated a Russian army near the Alma River. Then they
marched around the town of Sevastopol and dug in just to the
south, organizing their attack and shelling the city. This devastating siege would last for eleven months.

Leo's friend and coeditor, Komstadius, had just been ordered
to Sevastopol. The town had been steadily bombarded for weeks.
On October 24, in the battle of Inkerman Heights, Komstadius
died. Leo was heartsick at the loss of his friend. Yet here, in
Kishinev, a mad social whirl was in progress. The Tsar's sons
Grand Dukes Michael and Nicholas appeared at a local ball.
Gaiety reigned—while Sevastopol lay besieged a few hundred
miles away. Tolstoy could not reconcile that world of courage

51

and dying with the frenzied entertainment and the luxurious idling at Kishinev. He reported to Prince Gorchakov and requested permission to serve at Sevastopol. Gorchakov knew of Komstadius' death. He remembered the sample *Military Gazette* and Tolstoy's frank and brilliant stories of soldier life, and he granted the request to serve at the front.

Tolstoy, promoted to lieutenant, hurried to Sevastopol, almost afraid that he would arrive too late to help defend the city. As he entered the town on November 7, a regimental band on the boulevard was playing a lilting dance tune. The blue waters of the harbor sparkled in the sun, and flags flew gaily everywhere. However, from the defended southern outskirts, thunderous echoes sounded. Several shells screamed into the town itself, exploding in another area. Tolstoy strolled about the muddy, stinking streets, strewn with bombs and shot of various sizes. Throngs of soldiers, sailors, and civilians crowded the avenues. All went about their business among the ruined buildings and houses with a calm self-confidence, as though the powerful enemy at their doors did not exist. The young officer felt proud that he was part of this fearless people.

A military funeral slowly approached through the littered street. Tolstoy stepped aside and entered the Hall of Assembly, which had been turned into a busy hospital. The odor of death greeted him. He stooped and spoke with a cheerful old soldier who had lost his leg and was soon to be discharged. Groaning men lay all around on rude cots. Medics bustled through, bringing in more of the wounded. Nearby a young woman lay dying; she had been shot while carrying her sailor husband's dinner to him. Tired doctors were amputating in an adjoining area. The smell of chloroform filled the room. As the amputees regained consciousness their cries and curses tortured the air. Suffering was everywhere. Leaving the hospital, Tolstoy realized how little of battle he had experienced and how much less the world "outside" understood this horror. He determined to write the truth about the defenders of Sevastopol.

For a week he toured the forward defense fortifications which had been erected around the town. Every bastion was taking a deadly beating from the allies' shelling. Eighty French guns were trained on the Fourth Bastion. In a letter to Sergei he described the men he found there:

> The spirit among the troops is beyond any description. In the time of ancient Greece there was not so much heroism. Kornilov [the loved vice admiral], making the rounds of his troops, instead of hailing them with "Good health to you, lads!" says: "If you must die, lads, will you die?" and the soldiers shout: "We will die, your Excellency! Hurrah!"

Tolstoy was convinced that Sevastopol could not fall when it was defended by such men.

Having met some English and French prisoners, however, he was impressed with their strength and stature. The Russians seemed shrunken by comparison. Another truth jolted him: The allied infantrymen were armed with rifles, while the Russians carried old-fashioned muskets. He was also uncomfortably aware of the fact that many of the generals from his own army had been chosen not for proficiency or intelligence, but because they had friends at court or because their families were well known. In the reports Leo was given to compile, the Russian leaders' lack of military skill became sickeningly apparent. Still, he convinced himself that the determination of his countrymen would carry them through to victory.

For a few weeks in December his battery was quartered inland at Simferopol. He flirted with pretty young women, hunted red deer, and was surprised to find himself well liked by officers and men. Clowning around a piano one evening, he delighted them all by composing some witty couplets satirizing the high command and the war. The verses, set to an old tune, were a smashing success. Soon the whole army was singing these "Songs of Sevastopol." Leo squirmed in the dubious honor of this authorship. Hooting at one's betters was a rare and daring practice in that day. However, it had to be admitted that each ditty contained a sharp grain of truth.

In February Tsar Nicholas I died, and Russia was secretly

glad, for this ruler had been a bigoted despot who had increased his people's oppression. Perhaps his successor, Alexander II, would allow some of the needed reforms and ease the lives of the vast suffering peasant class. The siege of Sevastopol and the war in the Crimea continued in spite of the change of tsars.

Tolstoy kept at his writing each day that duty would permit. Praise had come pouring in for "Memoirs of a Billiard-Marker," which Nekrasov had at first hesitated to publish. Leo had dashed it off in four days before leaving the Caucasus. Now he was trying to finish *Youth*, a final follow-up to *Childhood* and *Boyhood*, but his pen kept straying to the stories of Sevastopol. In these sketches the young writer grasped the horrible skeleton of war, looked resolutely into its vacant eyes, then wrote honestly about what he had seen. His pride in the bravery of the Russian people at Sevastopol expressed itself in strong, realistic language.

When Tsar Alexander II read the first of these published sketches, "Sevastopol in December," he was genuinely moved by the plight of his soldiers. He ordered the story translated into French and published in a newspaper. His wife, the new young Empress, wept when she read the plain, open account of the siege, charged with details. No one before Tolstoy had told so clearly of war's brutality.

The part-time war correspondent would taste the bitterness of war, as well as observe and describe it. From April 3 to May 15, Tolstoy and his battery were ordered to the dangerous Fourth Bastion which caught the brunt of French firing. These six weeks were a confused nightmare. Here were the incessant thunder of cannon: the shouts of "Mortar!" and "Ca-an-non coming!"; the visiting priests who held crosses high and exhorted the weary men to fight to the end. Tolstoy faced the specter of death, when there was hardly time to carry off the bodies, and never a moment to change one's clothes, or wash or sleep. His senses absorbed the smell of powder, the moans of wounded and shell-shocked men, the sight of bombs like darting stars that tore human beings apart when they burst. He tasted the quickly-snatched battle rations which the stomach often rejected.

A single night of attacks and counterattacks often resulted in a

thousand dead and wounded on each side. Tolstoy found himself praising God for His protection. Inspired by the fighters around him, he showed great courage under the endless heavy firing. When he later won the Medal of St. Anne for his valor, he could only think of those brave defenders of Sevastopol.

In mid-May he was sent to form a mountain platoon on the banks of the Belbek, fourteen miles away. Sevastopol was in its eighth month of siege. The quiet of Tolstoy's new quarters seemed unearthly after the constant cannonade around the city.

Flattered by the Tsar's notice of "Sevastopol in December," Tolstoy was also delighted to receive a congratulatory letter from Turgenev, the famous author who was Marya's friend. But an army censor came to life and slashed honest "Sevastopol in May" to ribbons even after it was printed. The author was furious. The same government which had commended him was now forbidding him to speak. He had ended that story of Sevastopol with these words: "The hero of my tale, whom I love with all the power of my soul . . . is truth."

On August 4, 8,000 Russian soldiers died in battle on the Chernaya River. Tolstoy took part in this bloody encounter, but was called on for very little action. Unable to stay away from battle-weary Sevastopol, he kept riding into the town all summer, hoping to find that the siege had somehow been lifted. Each visit revealed more suffering. Finally, on August 28, 1855, his birthday, he arrived in time to observe the French charge Malakov Hill. The bombardment had gone on for twenty-four hours. As Tolstoy watched through a spyglass from high ground north of the city, the sounds of cannon were replaced with the staccato of rifle fire. He noticed soldiers racing through the ruined streets. He couldn't believe what he saw. The flag on Malakov—a French flag! The city was in flames. Blue, white, and red standards were being raised everywhere. Throngs of Russians were leaving by the pontoon bridge. Sevastopol had fallen. After eleven cruel months, the siege was over, and with it, the war.

The final, truthful results of the Crimean conflict would not be assessed until much later. Political gains for the victorious allies were meager. Russian warships were forbidden in the Black Sea, but only for a few years. Half a million lives had been lost, and the damages to property were worth millions of rubles. As for Tolstoy, he had fully decided that literature, not military life, was for him. In his search for truth he had also learned unforgettable lessons about war.

THE TRAVELING AUTHOR

The Crimean War was over, and the unconquered hero headed for St. Petersburg. The literary men of Russia were waiting to greet him. His sister's friend Turgenev, Russia's foremost novelist, embraced him, hailed him as a brother, and insisted that Tolstoy move in with him. The young author readily agreed; he had looked forward to meeting this man with his gentle ways and famous talent. Turgenev introduced him to their editor, the poet Nekrasov. Other staff members of *Contemporary*, poets, and journalists came calling, too, and admiringly accepted him.

These men of letters filled their correspondence and diaries with notes on the new arrival. "What a delightful and exceptional man. . . ." Turgenev bragged paternally. Nekrasov wrote, "Likable, energetic, unselfish . . . a real falcon! Perhaps an eagle!" "He's a first-class chap, and a true Russian officer, full of wonderful tales, but he hates empty words. . . . " said Alexander Druzhinin, a literary critic. The confident young visitor from the country became the toast of the intelligentsia in the Capital of All the Russias.

Soon the comments about the newcomer took on a hint of envy. "This slip of an officer will gobble us all up," the writer

Alexei Pisemsky warned his colleagues. "From the first moment I noticed in young Tolstoy an involuntary opposition to all commonly accepted opinion," Afanasi Fet, a poet, commented.

And Turgenev complained, "He is forever posing in front of us. . . . You can soak a Russian officer in lye for three days but you won't soak out his Junker arrogance. . . ." If there ever had been a shy bone in Tolstoy's body, there was no longer. Two months later, when his third wartime sketch, "Sevastopol in August," was published, it did not bear the humble author's initials, L. N., but his full name, Count Leo Tolstoy.

Tolstoy was seeking frivolity to forget the dreadful war. When Fet, the young poet and landowner, arrived in St. Petersburg to meet this writer who was the current rage, Turgenev received him in his drawing room, whispering that Tolstoy was asleep in the next room. "He has . . . gone off on a tangent," sighed the scented host. "Sprees, gypsies, and cards every night; then he sleeps like the dead until two o'clock in the day. I tried to restrain him, but I've given it up now." Fet left without meeting the guest from Yasnaya, but their friendship later took root and lasted for a long time. Tolstoy's feelings for Turgenev alternated from warm to cool. The two men shared a love of good literature and a desire to produce it, but their personalities clashed. Tolstoy was brash, frank, free, and untamed. Turgenev was poetic and civilized. Quarrels boiled up between them. Nekrasov, the editor, made desperate efforts to act as peacemaker, not wanting to lose the contributions of either writer.

In January, 1856, Leo was summoned to Orel. His brother Dmitri was dying of tuberculosis. Dmitri lay in a shabby room, coughing his life away. He seemed a pale, emaciated shadow with enormous eyes. Each breath was a rattling exertion. A kind, tousle-haired girl walked quietly about, bathing the patient's damp forehead and seeing to his wants. Sickroom odors permeated the air. Standing in the doorway, his well-groomed brother from the city lowered his eyes. Here was more truth than he could bear. Memories jarred him: Dmitri caring for the poor and the sick, visiting prisons; Dmitri urging the family in Kazan to attend church; the teasing nickname "Noah" he had endured; his abstinence.

"Leo," whispered a familiar voice. Aunt Tatyana rustled toward him from the shadows, touching his face with her small hand. Marya and her husband also hovered near. But Leo turned away. In the face of death he faltered, and longed only to get back to the flattering attention of St. Petersburg society. Not this depressing reality. After a few days he left Orel.

When Dmitri died three weeks later, Leo wrote briefly to Aunt Pelagya, "He died a good Christian. That is a great comfort to us all." But the brother on his deathbed was not lightly forgotten. Many years later Dmitri reappeared poignantly as Nicholas in Tolstoy's novel *Anna Karenina*.

At St. Petersburg Tolstoy found a sincere and fascinating friend in whom he was to delight for fifty years. Countess Alexandra Tolstoy was his father's cousin, and a maid of honor at court; she was attractive, unmarried, of a religious nature, and eleven years older than Tolstoy—almost forty! He was proud of her wit and her influence in high circles. She marveled at his talent, youthful energy, and good conversation. Had she been nearer his age, he might have married her, or, scared, he might have run away altogether. As it was, they safely and platonically enjoyed each other's lively company, correspondence, and opinions. He dubbed her "Granny," and the nickname stuck. It was a durable friendship.

Near Moscow he dined with a playmate from early days, Lyubov Islenyev. This was the girl he had pushed off a balcony in childish jealousy so long ago. At sixteen she had married Dr. Andrey Behrs of German extraction and now she showed off her family. A pleasant meal was served by her three pretty daughters. Lisa was twelve; Sonya, eleven; and Tanya, ten. "What dear, merry little girls!" Leo commented. They had been allowed to read *Childhood* and were now thrilled to entertain the author, a count, an old friend. As Lyubov jokingly reminded Leo of her fall from the balcony, it probably occurred to her that this childhood admirer might one day become a suitor for Lisa, her eldest daughter. But, unaware that he might be considered for such a role, the charming visitor soon waved good-bye to the Behrs family and continued homeward to his people.

There were rumors that the serfs of Russia would soon be

freed by a decree of the new Tsar, Alexander II. In the years away from Yasnaya, Tolstoy had been troubled many times about his relations to his serfs. Before leaving St. Petersburg in May, he had drawn up his own "project of a project" to free his serfs and lease them land, letting them pay rent for thirty years. After that the land would be theirs absolutely. He had called upon several officials and statesmen in the capital, aggressively explaining these ideas. The bureaucrats were dry and noncommittal. He growled in his diary, "Russia today . . . is all being changed; but to accomplish the changes there are old men who are . . . unfitted for the work." He began to doubt that the government seriously intended to free the serfs. He might have to lead the way himself.

His usual happy homecoming at Yasnaya was marred by unpleasantness. The house looked different without the central structure he had gambled away. Then there was the disappointing attitude of conservative Aunt Tatyana to his proposals for freeing his people. "You could not knock the injustice of serfdom into her head in a hundred years," he grumbled. Such misunderstandings were going on all over Russia. Emancipation was the topic of the day. Everyone was strongly for or against freeing the serfs. No one was neutral.

Tolstoy determined to go ahead with his plan in spite of official evasion and the disapproval of others, even Aunt Tatyana. The day after his arrival he gathered his serfs together. From farmlands and pastures the men came, wiping foreheads on ragged sleeves. An earthy muzhik smell pervaded the summer air as they assembled before the steps of the big house. Leaning on their spades and *sokhas*, they gazed at their master. Tolstoy cleared his throat and told very simply of the good future he was planning for them. With a feeling of personal pride, he explained his liberal offer about the land. The serfs lowered their eyes and shuffled their feet, mumbling. Tolstoy could not understand why they did not throw their caps into the air and shout, "Hurrah!" Perhaps they had failed to understand. He held another meeting. He decided to give them time to think. Again and again he met with groups of the field serfs. Maddeningly unresponsive, they only smiled and shook their heads, as the master made his terms more liberal and became more outraged at their failure to react. Did they not want their freedom? He had forgotten the ancient accumulation of obstinacy and ignorance. He himself failed to take into account the rumors which now surrounded the idea of emancipation.

At last Vasili, a house servant, enlightened him, explaining that the serfs were sure they would be freed at the time of the new Tsar's coronation this coming August, and that the land would be given them outright then. They thought their master's "deal" was a fraud to bind them by contract. Rumors were everywhere about the fabulous decrees the Tsar would make in August. Of course the peasants did not want to cooperate in Tolstoy's project. They had greater expectations. Why should they accept part of his land when they imagined they would be given all? Freedom was a word people who had been serfs all their lives could hardly understand. Their idea seemed to be, Yes, we are yours, but your land is ours! In disgust Tolstoy tossed his plans aside, at least for the moment.

In August the coronation of the Tsar came and went without the expected emancipation decree. But Tolstoy still hoped that Russia would be reformed by this administration—that trial by jury would be introduced, the serfs freed and given land, and censorship of the press relaxed. Aunt Tatyana said nothing about Leo's failure to communicate with the serfs, nor the defeat of his project to give them lands and freedom. But he felt the gentle woman's silent triumph; the old ways were prevailing. In her smile he sensed her saying, "I told you so." It was irritating. Serfdom and religion were the two subjects he and Auntie could not discuss together. Yet she was so pleasant and loving in every other way that they soon found themselves laughing and teasing, as close as ever.

A short story, "The Snowstorm," and a short novel, *Two Hussars*, had been published that spring and were well received. During the summer Tolstoy worked on *A Landlord's Morning*, drawing from his experiences with the serfs. He sorted old notebooks and corrected *Youth*. While memories of the Caucasus engulfed him, he started an important short novel, *The Cossacks*.

When September came, he went hunting in frozen mud and

caught cold. But a much more serious illness was ruining his peace of mind. Valerya Arsenyev, a frivolous, poorly-educated, but charming girl, lived a few miles from Yasnaya Polyana with her sisters and her governess. The ladies, in league with Aunt Tatyana, had decided that the Count needed a wife. Only Sergei advised against matrimony. Hoping to cool the affair, he scoffed at Valerya Arsenyev's pretentiousness and her passion for clothes. Tolstoy called on Valerya almost every day, took her to dances and dinners, observed her, and wrote her letters. Local gossips whispered that the two were surely engaged. Aunt Pelagya came visiting and rejoiced in the prospective match. Sometimes Leo was sure he was in love with Valerya; at other times he thought her unbearably stupid and shallow. He worried in his diary, "Valerya is a splendid girl, but she certainly does not please me. However, if we meet so often I may suddenly marry her."

At last, in November, the cowardly suitor hurried back to St. Petersburg, to symphonies, literary friends, and the sweet freedom of bachelorhood. At Yasnaya, Aunt Tatyana and the neighbors were disgruntled that there was to be no wedding. But Tolstoy had found he could manage his life without the pretty flirt.

A Landlord's Morning was very successful. The spoiled author was somewhat disappointed in the public's response to *Youth*, but he was delighted to hear that the Tsar had read and liked *Childhood*.

After the New Year, he decided to go to Paris. A trip abroad was considered necessary for a polished young nobleman's education. Besides, he wanted to visit Turgenev, who was living there now. There was no one with whom he so enjoyed arguing! He traveled without a servant and arrived in Paris about Carnival time in February of 1857, moving into a cold furnished apartment two doors away from his friend. Turgenev rushed him off to the Opera Costume Ball, the first of dozens. "Madness," Tolstoy commented. Nekrasov, their editor, was also there, looking rather gloomy over his prospects for keeping the peace between these two prima donnas of the Russian literary world. Elegant Princess Lvov, the niece of a St. Petersburg family, captivated the newcomer. "The Princess is so delightful," he admitted. "I like her very much and think I am a fool not to try to marry her." Turgenev, on the other hand, got on his nerves. The two authors would forever be fascinated by each other, but they could not get along. Tolstoy's diary recorded his growing irritation with the elder author:

> (February 14) Turgenev is a child. (March 5) No, I want to avoid him! . . . To be intimate with him is impossible. (March 25) He no longer talks but chatters; he believes neither in reason, in people, nor in anything.

Nevertheless, Tolstoy was enjoying Paris. He was impressed with the freedom of the French people, their joy of living, their art, cafes, and theaters. Visiting the museums, Versailles, and Fontainebleau, he realized the limitations of his own education. He was astonished to find the public library crammed with people. At the Hotel des Invalides, a home for the needy war veterans of France, he was shown through the ornate granite tomb of Napoleon. When the guide began to intone his set speech of praise to the little General, Tolstoy's anger rose. Bonaparte—that monster! He walked quickly away from the mausoleum, murmuring rudely, "Soldiers—animals trained to bite everybody."

In late March someone asked Tolstoy if he would like to attend an execution. A murderer had been sentenced to death. Tolstoy said no, but still, early on the appointed day, he found himself rising, dressing, and setting out. A damp chill pervaded the crowded Place de la Roquette. Towering above the hushed throng loomed the guillotine, its steel blade glinting in the early morning sun. Tolstoy felt his stomach churning, but somehow he could not turn away. The condemned man climbed the wooden steps of the platform, kissed the Bible that was held out to him, and slowly knelt in the required position. As the knife dropped swiftly, the watching crowd gasped in unison. A dull thud was heard; the man's head rolled into a waiting box. Overwhelmed by waves of nausea, Tolstoy staggered away. "How senseless!"

he muttered fiercely. The crowd separated, allowing him to pass, staring at him. He went back to his apartment, his head pounding. "I will never anywhere serve any government."

Two days later he was on his way to Switzerland, breathing the fresh clean air, smiling as he remembered his emotions while saying good-bye to Turgenev. He was also sad to leave the lovely Princess Lvov.

Waiting to greet him in a handsome villa overlooking Lake Geneva was his cousin Alexandra Tolstoy, who was staying with her elder sister. Leo felt that "Granny" must be the most pleasant woman alive. The pair spoke often of pure friendship and delighted in each other's company. When they discussed religion, Tolstoy began to reread the Gospels, and soon found himself praying for more faith. In her memoirs Alexandra would say of him, "We had the same general traits of character. We were both terrific enthusiasts and had searching minds, we truly loved good, but did not know how to go about accomplishing it properly. . . ." Together the charming wanderer and the beautiful fortyish maid of honor visited the village where Rousseau had lived. When Tolstoy left for a side trip to the Italian Piedmont, their conversations were prolonged by notes and verses sent by mail. "When near you," she wrote, "it was difficult not to feel happy. . . . When I see you I always . . . want to be a better human being. . . ." Little wonder he adored his "Granny."

As Tolstoy admired Roman ruins in little Italian towns, people, travelers and natives, spoke to his writer's eye and begged to be recorded. The sampling of mankind which caught his fascinated attention was jotted into the diary:

> A charming blue-eyed Swiss girl. . . . An idiot girl who gazed at the sky. . . . A consumptive Corsican. . . . A bad concert artist with excessively long hair. . . . A dull official rogue. . . . An angry black gentleman. An excessively rude office-keeper . . . poor fishermen. . . . Pretty servant girls. . . . A young Swiss inquisitive about Russia . . . a fair-haired Italian . . . a merry German guide. . . . A pretty tobacconist.

. . . An idiot in a Napoleonic hat . . . square-
cornered Germans . . . slender Parisian French-
men, stout stalwart Swiss. . . . A traveling school
of girls and boys with a rosy, perspiring, heavy-
jawed master.

Back in Lucerne, Tolstoy was pleased one night by the clear yodeling of a street singer. He persuaded the man to come and perform at his elegant hotel, the Schweitzerhof. Large crowds gathered at windows and balconies to enjoy the melodies, but not a piece of silver was tossed. Tolstoy was furious that such beautiful song should go unrewarded. He insisted that the musician share a bottle of wine with him. The singer followed his sponsor into the formal dining room reluctantly. A waiter sized up the shabby visitor with the guitar and offered them an inferior table in another room. Tolstoy became arrogant as he ordered the finest champagne for his trembling guest. The hotel guests stared. Three days later he put the whole painful incident into a story, "Lucerne," asking a timely question: Should civilized people recognize class distinctions?

It was time to go. Lingering several weeks in Germany to gamble, he returned by sea to St. Petersburg on July 30, 1857, and proceeded toward Yasnaya Polyana. He awoke early one day, and jotted into his diary, "A gray, dewy Russian morning—with birch trees—delightful!" But the nearer he came to home, the more backwardness he seemed to behold. He saw petty officials mistreating the old, the sick, and the poor. A policeman slyly demanded a bribe from him. At the station a peasant was being flogged. Everywhere there were disgusting displays of man's inhumanity. "In Russia, all is odious, odious, odious," he mourned. Would mankind ever, anywhere, learn to make friends with itself?

TEACHING AND LEARNING

Appalled by injustices on every side, Tolstoy determined to try to rectify things, at least in his own little corner of the world. Working with the serfs and teaching them appeared to be the only answer. In 1859 he decided to give up his writing in order to devote himself to his people. *Family Happiness* had just been published. It was praised by the critics, but despised now by its author. "I shall write no more fiction," he said in a letter to his friend Fet. Why should he produce stories to entertain the privileged, literate "few" of Russia? He had come to long with all his heart to reach, teach, and do for the "many."

Nicholas was amused to see Tolstoy out plowing the land, working with sincere absorption as he practiced his new theory that a master should labor with his serfs. Nicholas dashed off an amusing note describing the scene to Fet:

> Lyovotchka is delighted with the way the serf Ufan
> sticks out his arms when ploughing, and so Ufan
> has become for him an emblem of village strength

> . . . and he himself, sticking his elbows out wide,
> takes to the plow and "ufanizes."

Nicholas' laughter soon changed into a hacking cough. The oldest brother was far from well, but the robust youngest one could plow or mow with the strongest of his serfs, then visit with family and guests far into the night.

Turgenev saw Tolstoy at work in the fields, and mourned that his friend was "lost to literature." Conservative Fet also found little amusement in his friend's activities with scythe and plow. Like Aunt Tatyana and most other provincial aristocrats, Fet did not believe in emancipation and the changes it would bring. Even the serfs disapproved behind Tolstoy's back.

Friends and relatives who feared that Tolstoy had "gone over to the peasants" did not bother to comment on his relationship with a married peasant woman, Aksinia. To his diary he confessed that he was actually "in love" with Aksinia. Of course Aunt Tatyana was still on the lookout for a suitable girl for him to marry.

In September of 1858, Tolstoy had signed a petition requesting that each serf be freed and given land. The landowners were to be reimbursed by the government for the relinquished acreage. One hundred four nobles of his province of Tula signed with him, but they represented only a small number of the landlords. The others refused. And the petition was ignored by the government.

Tolstoy decided to establish another school for the peasant children. At this time, there was no public education in Russia. Only a few serfs could read or write. Leo remembered well the failure of his school in 1848, when the peasants had suspiciously kept their children away from the classroom. But now, eleven years later, emancipation was in the air, and many of his serfs were somehow guessing that the master's free school might actually benefit their young ones.

Twenty-two shy children were enrolled. Encouraged by the vigorous Count, they edged timidly into the big house and up the stairs to the schoolroom. Scrubbed and dressed in their pathetic best clothes, they raised frightened eyes to the stern portraits of ancestral Tolstoys on the walls. Tolstoy himself welcomed the

68

children and immediately began to practice his unique plan of instruction. His idea was to foster a love of learning in these young minds. In an educational magazine he described the pupils and the methods of his peasant school with obvious pride:

> No one brings anything with him, neither books nor copybooks. No homework is set them. Not only do they carry nothing in their hands, they have nothing to carry even in their heads. They are not obliged to remember any lesson, nor any of yesterday's work. . . . They bring only themselves, their receptive nature, and an assurance that it will be as jolly in school today as it was yesterday.

It was impossible to resist the happy originator of this unusual program, he was so interested in each student's progress. The children disciplined each other. An occasional noisemaker would meet sharp eyes on every side. "Sh!" they would hiss. "We can't hear anything! Stop it!" Tolstoy related:

> Sometimes teacher and pupils are so carried away that a lesson lasts three hours instead of one. Sometimes the pupils themselves cry: "Go on, go on!" and shout contemptuously to any who are tired: "If you're tired go to the little ones!"

He added later, "They fell in love with the book, and with learning, and with me. It only remained for me to guide them on. . . ." Under such tender teaching the shy children soon relaxed; the inhibited unwound; the "stupid" became amazingly alert. All learned. The Yasnaya Polyana School was a success.

Nicholas' cough seemed worse every day. He was pale, nervous, drank too much, and had grown so thin that his clothes no longer fit. Lately, visiting at Yasnaya Polyana, he had begun to wear a faded old uniform from the Caucasus. One May morning in 1860, he told his brother that he was going to stay for a while in Soden, Germany, where the waters were said to be good for the lungs. Leo paused. He had been hurrying up to the school, which now had an enrollment of fifty peasant children. Classes would soon be ended so that the youngsters could help with summer work in the fields. He looked anxiously at Nicholas, the person he respected more than anyone in the world. The gaunt man breathed with difficulty. Leo seemed to see a specter of the dying Dmitri. A cough tickled his own throat, which constricted with fear. The lung disease was galloping swiftly through those he loved. Was he, too, going to succumb? Was the whole family to give up and die of consumption just when there were so many important things to accomplish? He wrote to Fet, "I am oppressed by . . . the illness of Nikolenka. . . . I feel undone."

Sergei escorted their feverish brother to Soden. There a doctor advised him to try the warm air of Hyères in the south of France. Leo was summoned, and in late August, he and Nicholas, Marya, and her three children left by train for France. In Hyères, an old hillside town near the sea about fifty miles from Marseilles, Marya rented a villa overlooking the Mediterranean. Leo and Nicholas took rooms in a town house not far from a doctor. The sky shone blue above the ancient, winding streets. But though the air was delightful, the psychological atmosphere was dismal. The town was filled with the sick and dying. Like Nicholas, they had been sent here by doctors; Hyères' fine climate was their last hope.

Nicholas insisted on dressing and caring for himself, though he soon became too weak to leave the house. He was embarrassed when he was found coughing blood into a pan, and finally began to accept assistance. He would smile faintly at his brother, murmuring with troubled breathing, "Thanks, friend." His large glittering eyes followed Tolstoy around the stuffy room. The damp face against the pillow was haggard and touchingly familiar. Feeling frantic, Tolstoy waited on the patient tactfully. While thoughts of death ran through his head, he sat by the sickbed, speaking softly and tenderly of old times, happy days, Papa, of the green stick, of the Caucasus and friends. The end came much sooner than he or his sister expected. Marya had made her daily visit to them on September 20, 1860. As she was leaving, Leo walked with her to her carriage. When he returned

to the bedroom, Nicholas was unconscious. Tolstoy was about to go for the landlady, the doctor—anyone!—when his brother suddenly opened his eyes, stared wildly about, and sputtered, "What is that?" Soon after, he was dead.

In Hyères' walled burial ground ancient tombstones crumbled under heavy tropical vines. A few friends accompanied the small family of mourners to Nicholas' grave. After the brief Orthodox service Tolstoy wrote in his diary, "This event [has] torn me away from life. Again the question: Why?" More than ten years later he still brooded on the undecipherable "Why" of his brother's death as he wrote in *A Confession*:

> Wise, good, serious, he . . . died painfully, not understanding why he had lived and still less why he had to die. No theories could give me, or him, any reply to these questions during his slow and painful dying.

The sad little family stayed on in Hyères a while longer. The sick surrounding them seemed strangely like relatives now. "Wherever one goes," Marya wrote to a friend, "there are the sick. . . . A congress of dying consumptives!" Tolstoy moved into the villa with his sister and her lively children. At a writing table with a view of the sea he resumed work on *The Cossacks* and started an article on education.

Marya's bright youngsters adored "Uncle Leo." After dinner he would delight them with gymnastics, invented games, or spontaneous operas. Or he would teach them. One evening after developing their muscles for a while doing stunts, he tried to exercise their brains. "What is the difference between Russia and other countries?" he asked, and ordered, "Write here, in my presence, and nobody is to copy from anybody else!" The children struggled and scrawled. At last the papers were presented. One said that Russia was different because people ate blinis during Shrovetide and went out tobogganing, and that at Eastertime Russians liked to dye eggs. For another Russia meant snow; for the third, a troika with three fine horses. "Bravo," applauded the teacher. As a reward he brought watercolors from

Marseilles and painted with them. But his mind kept straying to the peasant classroom at Yasnaya. In a letter which typified his thoughts at the time, he urged his Auntie, "Tell the teacher to send me news about the school." Perhaps he should head back home to his peasants.

He traveled for two months in Italy, sightseeing, then decided to continue researching educational techniques abroad. He had already visited Marseilles to study eight state schools. In an article published some time later, "On Public Education," he reported that the French schools, like those in Germany, crushed the inquisitive nature of the child by harsh discipline and teaching by rote, but that the theaters, museums, cafes, and popular French literature added up to an excellent education from life. After a brief return to Hyères, he traveled to Paris. Greeting his friend Turgenev, Tolstoy soon dashed off to interview students and teachers in a lycée. Two weeks later he arrived in London in time to hear a favorite author, Charles Dickens, lecture on education. He examined the much-admired English methods of education first-hand in the classrooms.

In March 1861, as he was leaving London for Brussels, a newspaper headline caught Tolstoy's eye: "Emancipation of the Russian Serfs." It had come at last. After centuries of oppression Russia's serfs were free. The news moved him profoundly. He thought about going straight home to be with his people, but decided to continue to Belgium. His mind was busy with the terms of the Tsar's decree, which had been proclaimed in Russia in February but were only now being announced in England. Landowners and serfs were placed under certain restrictions until 1863, when the serfs would be freed absolutely. They could then borrow money from the government to purchase part of the land they had worked. All these terms had been read aloud to the serfs in the stately, legalistic language of the government. Most of the listeners probably understood little. Sergei wrote to his brother on March 12, 1861:

> These are fascinating days. The emancipation manifesto was read out to the people, who did not

> pay close attention, and it seems to me they are all
> rather dissatisfied. . . . I offered to explain it all
> to the peasants at Yasnaya Polyana . . . but
> nobody seemed to want me to do so.

On the strength of Sergei's letter and his own experiences with
the peasants, Tolstoy wrote to a Russian journalist he had met in
England:

> The muzhiks are all dissatisfied. Before, they could
> hope that everything would turn out all right; now
> they know for certain that everything will be all
> wrong, at least for the next two years. . . .

And in his notebook he declared, "My one aim is education of
the masses."

Near Brussels, Tolstoy called on the remarkable political
writer Pierre Joseph Proudhon. This simple, pleasant man had
written that the ideal society would be the one with the least
government. He showed Tolstoy his new treatise on war between
nations, which was called *War and Peace*. The traveler discussed
the recent emancipation with this philosopher. Tolstoy declared
that the upper classes in Russia were interested not only in
freeing the serfs, but in educating them. "Is it possible that this is
really true?" Proudhon asked. "If this is true," he said almost
enviously, "the future belongs to you Russians."

In each country he visited, Tolstoy studied schools and bought
books on education. The interesting idea of marrying and beginning a family of his own intruded into his thoughts almost as
frequently as emancipation and the art of teaching. At the age of
thirty-two, he found himself ready to fall in love, if the right girl
would just appear and be willing. But, he wrote Sergei regarding
matrimony, "I don't have much hope left on that score, because
my last remaining teeth are crumbling to bits. But my spirits are
high!" In April he headed for Russia; he was never to leave his
homeland again.

On the train to St. Petersburg he considered Princess Golit-
sin's niece who lived in Hyères. In the capital he discussed his

problems with his cousin "Granny," and called on Princess Lvov. In Moscow he danced with refined Katerina Tyutchev, a poet's daughter, and visited again the charming Behrs family. When this family was not staying at their country home, they lived in an apartment in the Kremlin, where Dr. Behrs served as court physician. Tolstoy was pleased by their vivacious life style. The daughters had grown up now and were even prettier. Bookish Lisa, the oldest, was of marriageable age at seventeen. Of the three girls, she was probably the most intelligent. Sonya, sixteen, was romantic and dreamy; young Tanya was lively and teasing. Tolstoy found himself more marriage-minded after each of his visits to this family.

Returning to Yasnaya Polyana, he embraced Aunt Tatyana and talked with her in French. Then he raced up to visit his school. Joyful shouts from the peasant children greeted him. All wanted to touch him, kiss his hands, ask him questions, gain his attention in one way or another. They remembered the school as having been much more fun under the Count than with their present teacher. Leo recognized each child. Taraska. Danilka, grown so tall. Syomka and Fyodka. He had forgotten none of them. They were so glad that he had returned. There was a bond of love between teacher and students.

The next meeting was somewhat more difficult. The field serfs had been called together on the steps of the master's house. They bowed politely, but eyed their master with the same old hostility. Tolstoy explained the terms of the recent emancipation. Then he told how he was permitting them the maximum acreage allowed under the law, eight acres per person. This would leave him only around 1800 of his original 4000 acres. The peasants murmured thanks, bobbing their heads subserviently. They showed little enthusiasm for the master's beneficence.

In March, while Tolstoy was still in Brussels, he had been appointed "arbiter of the peace" by the governor of his home province of Tula. His job was to settle disputes between the emancipated peasantry and their former masters. There had been an immediate quarrel over his appointment. The minister of the interior received a petition of complaint asking that Tolstoy's appointment be revoked, on the grounds that he was known to be too lax with his own serfs. But the Governor of Tula insisted that the Count was widely respected and "a well-educated man."

During the next year Tolstoy labored at the thankless task of being a fair peacemaker. He pleased no one, and almost ruined his digestion. The landowners were indignant when he ruled against them. They denounced him to the authorities and even wrote him threatening letters. The serfs, on the other hand, would come to him in pitiful fashion when he ruled in favor of the nobility. "Do something, little father. . . . Have pity on us. . . . If you wanted to, you could fix it. . . ." To be fair and honest, to seek the truth as he had done in his writings, now seemed impossible. He wished to escape again to the private world of creating literature, or to the satisfying role of school-master. In April, 1862, he resigned the unenviable position, "arbiter of the peace."

While juggling disputes and wrangles between master and serf, he had managed to found fourteen peasant schools in the district. All used Tolstoy's methods of instruction. He coached the young teachers himself. They were excited by his novel ideas, by his enthusiasm, and simply by the Count himself. One day several teachers confessed that they had come to the country full of revolutionary notions. Their plan had been to stir the peasantry into revolt. But after delving into Tolstoy's idea for educating the masses they burned their subversive literature and turned to what seemed a nobler cause.

The school at Yasnaya Polyana was now located in a two-story building. The two classrooms were painted pink and blue, and there were two rooms for teachers. A large hall served as a public museum. Tolstoy felt he must share with the world some of his fascinating pedagogical discoveries, and so began the *Yasnaya Polyana* magazine. It ran twelve issues between February, 1862 and March, 1863. Tolstoy filled it with articles and notes on the art of instruction. Some of his theories were based on his extensive studies of the schools abroad. Most of his ideas, however, were the result of his successful educational experiments among the children of the fields of Yasnaya.

LOVE AND MARRIAGE

In Moscow the Behrs family entertained each evening. A lighted candle in the window of their large, old-fashioned apartment in the Kremlin indicated that the family was at home and would be pleased to receive guests. Servants bustled about the dim dining room, setting the substantial table with extra places for those who cared to stay for supper. A cheery samovar steamed. In the crowded reception rooms, songs, laughter, charades, and piano melodies mingled discordantly. Occasionally the young people put on amateur theatricals. Everyone enjoyed these gatherings, which were capably supervised by Lyubov Behrs.

There were five Behrs sons, whose friends visited the three charming Behrs daughters. Lisa had matured into a cool intelligent beauty; graceful Sonya's dark eyes held a knowing allure; and young Tanya had become a flirt with a lovely voice. Mrs. Behrs saw that her spirited girls were modest and proper, but she also helped to make eligible suitors welcome. One young man, Mitrofan Polivanov, a member of the Horse Guards, was already devoted to the middle sister. Before leaving Moscow he had asked her to wait for him. Sonya had smiled encouragement to the guardsman.

Moscow seemed remarkably interesting to Tolstoy that winter of 1862. In a rented apartment he spent many hours expounding his theories of education for his magazine, *Yasnaya Polyana*, which had miraculously been approved by the government censor. This unusual schoolmaster suggested for the classroom that "external disorder is useful and necessary, however strange and inconvenient it may seem to the teacher," and "There is only one criterion in teaching: freedom!"

To divert his mind he frequently visited the popular Behrs family. Lyubov, his childhood friend, made him comfortable, sending her lovely oldest daughter to greet him. "Lisa Behrs tries to tempt me," he noted in his diary.

Relatives and friends assumed that the Count was courting Lisa. One night after supper Tanya whispered to her sister, "Sonya! Just see how Lisa is sugaring up to Leo. . . ." The whole family welcomed and flattered Tolstoy. Dr. Behrs and the boys proved a fascinated audience for his tales of the Crimean War. Lisa and Sonya played piano duets with him and begged for news of his peasant schools. Through private study with tutors, both girls had earned teachers' certificates, although their ambitions seemed to run more to marriage than to teaching. The Count invited serious Lisa to contribute an article to his pedagogical magazine. Tanya sang for him, read poetry with him, and teased him into clowning at parlor games.

When Tolstoy returned to Yasnaya Polyana in the spring, he found himself missing those girlish voices. A cough was also bothering him. Nicholas and Dmitri seemed to hover near. Would he be the third brother stricken with consumption? He rushed back to Moscow to Dr. Behrs. The physician recommended a trip to Samara, the ancient southland east of the Volga River. The air of the Russian steppes would do him good. And the native *kumys*, a drink of fermented mare's milk, would calm his nerves and heal his body.

When the Behrses learned that Tolstoy was to travel to Samara for his health, it was Sonya who prayed for a long time before the icon in her bedroom. Observant little Tanya whispered in the candlelight, "Sonya, do you love the Count?"

78

Almost inaudibly, she replied, "I don't know." Then, "Oh, Tanya, two of his brothers died from consumption!"

"What if they did?" comforted Tanya. "He has quite a different constitution. You may be sure that Papa knows better than we do."

The primitive wilderness of Samara was good for the ailing author. He lived in a felt tent, drank the prescribed *kumys*, and relaxed in body and soul. For hours he discussed religion with the nomad people of the steppe. At this safe distance from the interesting Behrs girls, he dreamed of love and a happy, virtuous married life.

When he set out for home in July, his spirits were high and his health splendid. Upon reaching Yasnaya, however, he was handed the news that his house had been searched by the police. They seemed to suspect him of revolutionary activity. Of course, the constables' search had proved negative. They had found no secret passageways nor telegraphic equipment, only a new-fangled camera in the school. Poor Aunt Tatyana had protested weakly. At last the police had departed to report that the Count evidently had no plans to overthrow the government.

Tolstoy was furious. He soon poured out the whole story to the Behrs family. "They rummaged through everything . . . read aloud my private diaries and my most personal letters," he exploded. "My name has been dishonored. . . . I cannot live in Russia! I must leave everything and go abroad!"

"This will all blow over," soothed Dr. Behrs, "and you must stay here to see it through." Granny also begged Tolstoy to do nothing rash, but to seek God's help and to forgive the offense. He cooled off and decided to stay in Russia. He could hardly tear himself away at this time, anyway, for his life was swiftly assuming a new dimension.

In late July, 1862, Mrs. Behrs decided to take her daughters to see her old father at his country estate. On the way she planned to visit her friend, Tolstoy's sister, Marya, who was staying at Yasnaya Polyana. Perhaps the Count would also be at home. After spending the night in Tula, the excited group in the Behrs carriage turned up the avenue of lime trees. The girls were looking especially pretty. Each one secretly hoped that the eligible Count would fall in love with her. Marya and Tatyana greeted the travelers, embracing each and exclaiming over the girls. Tolstoy gaily ushered the travelers around his large estate. Lyubov Behrs was sad to find that part of the old house had been sold and removed. But Lisa's cool eyes were shining, and sentimental Sonya suddenly became a witty conversationalist. Tanya astonished her mother by assuming the grown-up airs of a lady of fashion.

The visiting family was given the ground-floor room with the vaulted ceiling. Lyubov Behrs sent Sonya to help the maid make up the beds. To Sonya's surprise the Count came along to assist them. Years later she still recalled her feelings as she watched him awkwardly unfold the sheets. "I felt a little embarrassed," she said, "but at the same time there was something nice and intimate in the way . . . he helped us to arrange the beds."

When supper was announced, Sonya had disappeared. Tolstoy found her sitting alone on the balcony, admiring the view of the hills in the twilight. "No, thank you, I don't want to eat," she said when he invited her to come inside. "It's so fine out here."

The Count joined his guests in the dining room, but soon he returned to the girl on the balcony. She smiled shyly. In the mellow light he appeared graceful and tall, like a storybook lover. He seated himself beside her and said softly, "How serene and simple you are. . . ." The fragrance of summer surrounded them.

The next day friends and neighbors joined the Tolstoy family and their guests on a carriage drive to a grassy meadow. The host invited Sonya to ride the splendid gray mare. "Yes, but I haven't a riding habit," she protested, indicating her dainty yellow dress.

"That doesn't matter," he assured her. "There are no villas here; no one except the trees of the wood will see you." He lifted her into a sidesaddle; then he mounted a white stallion. The couple cantered smartly together to the green picnic spot, while Lisa Behrs watched them from her place in the carriage.

House servants supervised hampers and boxes of specially-prepared food. An ice-cream container was unloaded by the cook's helper. A samovar was unpacked from straw and set steaming on a colorful table. In the meadow the friends relaxed, delighting in the scenery, the food, and the cheerful company. The Count seemed everywhere at once. After lunch, at Marya's suggestion, all the young people climbed a huge haystack and began to sing rounds and country songs, interrupted by laughter and a final hay slide.

The next day the guests from Moscow departed to Lyubov's father's estate. An afternoon or two later, Tanya was sitting on the veranda with her grandfather when they noticed a vigorous, bearded traveler approaching on a white horse. She ran upstairs to tell Sonya and Lisa, "The Count is coming."

"No! Really?"

"Is he alone?" Prettying themselves, the three girls came down to greet their visitor. Rather dingy from his warm three-hour ride, Tolstoy entered the rambling country house. The host, Alexander Islenyev, insisted that Tolstoy remain overnight. Tanya was chattering nonsense. Even Lisa became animated, introducing the distinguished guest to several visitors. But Sonya lowered her large luminous eyes, sure that she was the inspiration for the Count's long ride.

That night after the dancing, when most of the company had left, Grandfather suggested that Tanya sing for them. She refused and went into the parlor where, on impulse, she hid under the piano. The family forgot her, resuming their conversation.

Later, when the group was dispersing to retire, Tolstoy caught Sonya's hand and whispered, "Wait a minute, Sonya!" With a boyish air, he seated her at an open card table in the empty room. They did not notice Tanya, still hidden under the piano, and trapped now in her vantage point. She felt she should reveal her presence, but was ashamed to do it. The card table at which Tolstoy and Sonya sat had been covered with fresh green felt. A piece of chalk was handy for scorekeeping. Tolstoy hesitated before daring to speak to Sonya. "Try to read what I'll write, " he commanded. "Y.y.a. . . . h.r.m.t.v.o.m. . . . a. . . ." It looked like a code.

Sonya gave a puzzled laugh. "Impossible!" Then, somehow, with Tolstoy's willing assistance, she was able to decipher the

sentence. "Your youth and . . . happiness remind me too vividly of my . . . age. . . . ." He nodded.

"Well, let's try again." And he scribbled, "I.y.f.e.a.f.i.a.t.m. a.y.s.L."

Eyes shining, she translated in a whisper, "In your family exists a false idea as to me and your sister Lisa."

He looked at her fondly and wanted to write again, but her mother's voice sounded sternly from above. "Sonya!" She skimmed away upstairs, where she confided the whole incident to her diary. Tolstoy, alone again at the card table, probably did not even hear the sound on the other side of the room as Tanya, the eavesdropper, slid quickly from under the piano and hurried out, leaving behind a realistic writer in a romantic fog.

The next day the youngest sister found Lisa crying. "Tanya," she sniffed, "Sonya is taking Leo . . . away from me. Haven't you noticed it? . . . The finery she has decked herself out in, those glances she gives him, the pains she takes to be alone with him—all those things are as clear as day to everyone."

By the end of summer Tolstoy was staying in Moscow and visiting the Behrses almost daily. Family friends still thought the Count was Lisa's suitor. Even Dr. Behrs refused to believe that Tolstoy's choice was Sonya. But the sensitive girl somehow understood that she would probably be Countess Tolstoy one day, the wife of a famous man.

The famous man writhed with indecision. The idea of marrying Sonya obsessed him. But should he give up his freedom? Take on a wife at his age? And could she possibly return his love? His diary reveals his turmoil:

> (August 23, 1862) I'm afraid of myself: what if it is only the desire for love again and not love itself?
> (August 28, his birthday) I am thirty-four years old. . . . Got up with my usual feeling of depression. . . . Ugly mug. Give up any thought of marriage. Your vocation is elsewhere. . . .
> (August 29) Delicious night. Good, comfortable feeling. . . . I was confused. She too.

(September 5) In the evening we talked of love. From bad to worse.

(September 7) Don't go poking your nose into youth and poetry and beauty and love. There are cadets for that, old man. . . .

(September 8) I am irresistibly drawn to her.

(September 12) I am in love as I did not believe it possible to be. I am insane.

(September 13) Tomorrow I shall go and speak out or else I shall kill myself.

Two days later, leaving the Kremlin, he felt like a boy as he whispered to Sonya that he had something important to tell her—tomorrow. And he fled.

On September 16 Tolstoy arrived at the Behrs home with a letter heavy in his pocket. Tanya had been singing. Sonya, pale and agitated, was at the piano. Lisa looked tense. "Tanya, come try the waltz," suggested Sonya. "I think I've learned the accompaniment." Tanya began Arditi's "Il bacio," but Sonya's fingers moved clumsily and she struck several wrong notes.

Tolstoy replaced Sonya at the keyboard. Following along with the lovely song, he made a nervous wager with himself. "If she takes that final high note well, then I shall deliver my letter today. If she does it badly, I shan't deliver it." The melody swelled and ebbed. Tanya's ending to the song came through clearly and perfectly. Tolstoy waited. Tanya went to light the samovar. Lisa too had vanished.

He handed Sonya a white envelope. "Here is a letter that I've been carrying in my pocket for several days. Read it. I shall wait here for your answer."

She took the letter, hurried to her room, and locked the door. Her dark eyes moved over the long confession of love, suffering, and indecision, at last reaching the tortured proposal: "Will you be my wife? If you can say 'yes,' *boldly,* with all your heart, then *say it;* but if you have the faintest shadow of a doubt, say 'no.'" A knock at the door interrupted her.

"Sonya!" Lisa called. "Open this door, open it at once! I must see you. . . ." Sonya opened the door, holding the letter. "Sonya, what has the Count written to you? Tell me!"

"He has proposed to me," Sonya answered calmly.

"Refuse him!" Lisa was hysterical. "Refuse him instantly!" Then Mrs. Behrs appeared. She reproached Lisa and sent Sonya upstairs to answer her proposal. The radiant girl returned to the room where her awkward lover stood propped against the wall.

"Well?" he hardly dared ask aloud.

"Of course—yes," she said. Tolstoy's eyes filled with tears. Immediately Tanya, her mother, and all the servants came crowding in to join the jubilant couple. Lisa lingered in her own room. In his office Dr. Behrs sulked too. He felt that his oldest daughter should be married first, according to convention, and he blamed Tolstoy that Lisa was still unpromised.

A party had already been planned for the following day, September 17. Mrs. Behrs was celebrating her own and Sonya's saints' day. The house was filled with flowers and friends. As guests stepped forward one by one to congratulate her, Lyubov could not resist saying, "You may also congratulate us on the occasion of our daughter's betrothal." The visitors invariably turned to Lisa to wish her happiness. Lisa would redden and explain that Sonya was the bride-to-be.

When Mitrofan Polivanov, the cadet from the Horse Guards, stepped into the receiving line, he spoke to Mrs. Behrs, nodded to Lisa, then muttered bitterly to Sonya, "I knew that you would not stay true to me; I felt it." Tolstoy watched. Sonya was his. Even Lisa had forgiven him. Let the Horse Guards rant and rave; a terrifying happiness had invaded his soul.

Instead of allowing Sonya or her mother to set the date for the marriage, Tolstoy surprised the family by ordering that the wedding take place within a week, on September 23, 1862. While Dr. Behrs sputtered, his wife protested that a proper trousseau could hardly be prepared that quickly.

"Surely she's got enough clothes," insisted the placid bridegroom. "She's always perfectly well dressed." He was adamant. They were no match for him, so wedding plans went swiftly forward.

For Tolstoy, marriage and family living had always represented a unique state of virtue. He realized that his present joy
was due to Sonya. But there was also a strange feeling that his
old goals of self-perfection would somehow be achieved through
marriage. He was putting aside the illicit sensual pleasures of the
past. A few days before the wedding he made a strange request
of his fiancée. He asked her to read his old diaries, including the
records of his past sins and repentances. When he delivered the
journals to her, he felt a peculiar relief, as of a duty accom-
plished. To sheltered eighteen-year-old Sonya, on the other hand,
the diaries' frank and vivid descriptions of Tolstoy's bachelor life
were a devastating revelation. She was horrified as she turned the
closely scribbled pages. Only a few years ago he had written that
he was in love with a peasant woman. Years later Sonya admitted, "I remember how terribly shocked I was by the reading
of these diaries that he gave to me before my marriage out of a
sense of personal duty. . . . Wasted honesty! I shed many tears
over that look into his past." She cried bitterly that week and
slept little. But she could not back out; he might marry Lisa.

After six days of preparation, the breathless girl was ready for
the ceremony, dressed in a cloudlike gown and white veil.
According to Russian custom a groomsman was to appear at the
bride's home to give notice that her husband-to-be was waiting at
the church. The appointed hour came and went, then another
hour. Still no messenger. Sonya began to cry, wondering if
Tolstoy had changed his mind. At last she consented to sit,
careful not to wrinkle her elaborate dress. Just then Alexis,
Tolstoy's manservant, knocked at the door. He was apologetic.
"I forgot to keep out a clean shirt for the Count. . . . I'll have
to take a trunk down from the top of the carriage. I've come to
get a lantern." The family breathed in relief. At least the bridegroom had not run away; he merely needed a fresh shirt for the
wedding. Finally the correct trunk and the shirt were produced.

Soon the groomsman arrived to say that Tolstoy was waiting
for his bride at the church. The Behrses and their servants all
began to cry. Tears streaming down her face, Sonya was blessed
by her mother with the icon of St. Sofya the Martyr. Her father
kissed her; then, pleading illness, he limped down the hall to his

office. Leaving her parents behind as tradition dictated, Sonya went alone in a carriage for the ceremony at the Palace Church of the Nativity of the Virgin nearby, where Tolstoy and his friends awaited. Tolstoy looked formal and rather grim. "I felt . . . absolutely nothing," wrote Sonya later. "It seemed to me that something . . . inevitable was happening—nothing more."

Champagne and congratulations followed at the Behrs apartment. More tears. Then in silence all prayed for the couple's journey. With the rain pelting down on their coach in the darkness, they set out, accompanied by Alexis and by Sonya's old nurse, nicknamed "The Oyster." The sobbing bride and her husband spent the night at an uncomfortable inn. Arriving at Yasnaya Polyana the next day, they were embraced by Aunt Tatyana, who held a sacred icon high above their heads. Sonya turned from Auntie's arms to be greeted by her brother-in-law, blue-eyed Sergei, offering them bread and salt, the traditional emblems of Russian hospitality. A swarm of servants stepped shyly forward, bowing and congratulating their master and welcoming the pretty new Countess.

As usual, Tolstoy shared his feelings with his diary that evening: "Incredible happiness!"

"WAR AND PEACE"

In an affectionate letter to Fet, the new husband exulted, "I've been married for two weeks and am happy, and a new, entirely new man!" The couple quickly settled into the routine of country living. Tolstoy started to keep bees. He supervised seining the pond for carp, planted an apple orchard, and dismissed some stewards whose production was lagging. Rather untidy in his own habits, he nevertheless demanded that the pigsties be kept clean.

Sonya, after her whirlwind engagement, felt a new isolation. She was a city girl, accustomed to a lively house full of young people. Here, when Leo was away hunting or shut into his study writing, there were only ancient Aunt Tatyana, the servants, and a few callers. To relieve the boredom, she began to assume her share of the estate management. In no time a hundred duties vied for her attention, from the keeping of accounts to pickle-making. A bunch of household keys hung at her waist, which had just begun to thicken with pregnancy.

Despite Tolstoy's joy in marriage, he felt restless. The nature of this impulsive, insatiable man was to involve himself in vast efforts. The trifling, practical matters of the farms soon began to annoy him. He had lost interest in the peasant school. And now it seemed he could not write. He berated himself for idleness. *"I must work."* Was his childish, sometimes weepy doll-wife the cause of this irritability? "I'm happy with her," he scribbled in his diary, "but I am terribly dissatisfied with myself."

Intermittent quarrels erupted between the immature bride and the moody master of the house. Both were jealous. Faithful Tolstoy feared Sonya's flirtatious nature; the diaries of his past haunted her. She brooded in the oppressive country quiet that his old love affairs might continue. The sight of Tolstoy's former mistress, a simple peasant scrubwoman, brought a murderous gleam to Sonya's eye. She wrote fiercely in her diary, "A fat peasant, a vulgar woman. . . . It's ghastly! . . . I am quite simply losing my mind." Even Tolstoy's correspondence with Granny and Tanya's visits could needle the newly pregnant wife with doubt. In her own diary Sonya poured out her resentments and suspicions. Since she usually wrote in anger, she produced a volume of venom and despondence which misrepresents the couple's real devotion to each other. Tolstoy's diary of the time indicates that these early years of marriage were mostly a time of family happiness.

In January, 1863, *The Cossacks* finally came out. A year earlier Katkov, the publisher, had advanced gambling money to the author for the rights to this short novel about the Caucasus. Katkov profited heavily, for the striking, popular story was Tolstoy's best work so far. In its pages Epishka, Maryanka, and Sado come to life, as well as the spirit of the mountain region. In February "Polikushka" was published. Dr. Behrs was openly pleased with his son-in-law's successes. Turgenev lauded both works, in spite of the continuing quarrel between the writers.

Sunny days brought many guests to Yasnaya Polyana; they often stayed for weeks. Sergei and Marya visited often, as did Dyakov, Fet, and their wives. Best of all, delightful, animated Tanya appeared. "Our dear Tanya will come with the grasshoppers," predicted Aunt Tatyana. She was correct almost every summer.

As the weather warmed, Tolstoy wrote Marya, "I, happy man, still live. I listen to my child's kicking in Sonya's belly." The black leather couch on which all of the Tolstoy children had been born stood waiting in her room. On June 27 a physician and a midwife were hastily summoned from Tula. As Sonya screamed again and again, her helpless husband watched. The air was heavy with the smell of vinegar, candle tallow, and perspiration. Hours later, limp from weeping, Tolstoy heard the Polish doctor announce that a boy had been born. They named him Sergei.

The new father had his own ideas about the care of infants, as he did on almost every subject. He did not hesitate to insist on his own methods. The parents argued over the feeding of their colicky son. Sonya finally appealed to Dr. Behrs, who railed that his son-in-law might be a master of literature, but that he needed some common sense knocked into his head.

Accepting this wisdom, Tolstoy temporarily abstained from supervising the nursery. He felt unnecessary and unneeded; but a creative fever was smoldering in him. "The epic type would be a natural one for me," he thought. He toyed with profound ideas, and wrote to a friend:

> The aim of an artist is . . . to compel one to love life. . . . If I were told that . . . what I wrote would be read twenty years from now by those who are children today, and that they would weep and laugh over it and fall in love with the life in it, then I would dedicate all my existence and all my powers to it.

That summer an interesting interplay took place among their younger guests. Tolstoy the novelist missed none of it. Two of Tanya's suitors came visiting with her. Alexander Kuzminsky was a rather dull cousin; Anatol Shostak was an engaging, flashy scamp. The three of them filled Yasnaya with a flirtatious atmosphere which Sonya found very pleasant. Her husband made a few notes on the conversations of the young people. Tanya would make an appealing heroine for a novel. Yes, a girl with Tanya's sparkle and Sonya's romantic warmth. His energetic imagination was slowly beginning to work again. Like an artist who is preparing to paint a portrait, he began to observe his spontaneous sister-in-law.

"Tanya," he asked one day, "do you ever think of death?"

"No, but why are you asking me?"

"Someday you will die!"

"Me die? Never!" She wrinkled her nose and went off to join her friends. And in the writer's mind a fictional girl endowed with Tanya's joy of living took shape.

In October, 1863, officials in Tula planned a glittering ball for the Tsar's son Alexander, who was visiting their provincial town. Sonya was ill and refused to appear in public. So Tolstoy invited Tanya to attend the royal event. Sonya herself stitched an elegant white gown for her sister. Later the girl's fears, shy dignity, and wild delight in the ball were ascribed to the character of Natasha in Tolstoy's greatest novel.

Tolstoy's plans for *War and Peace* originally tended toward a historical theme. Now he knew there must be a panorama of human living as well, including birth, marriage, death, good and evil, the simple and the profound, peace and war. He would crowd all this against a vivid background of real history. No Russian novelist had written about the suffering of 1812 and the heroic victory over Napoleon, which only the magnificent determination of the Russian people had made possible. If only he could get it down on paper. He wrote to Dr. Behrs asking for diaries, old letters, newspapers, memoirs—any reference materials he could find covering the years 1805 to 1812. Bookish Lisa was pressed into service. She and her father responded with long lists of the available source material.

Glancing through the window at his icy lands one drab day, Tolstoy wrote Fet:

> You cannot imagine how hard I find the preliminary labor of plowing deep the field in which I must sow. To consider and reconsider all that may happen to all the future characters in the very large work I am preparing, and to weigh millions of possible combinations . . . is terribly difficult.

For the next six years he would concentrate his mental strength, great talent, and crowded hours on creating an epic work from the history of Russia and the Russian people.

By September, 1864, three-dimensional characters were coming to life on Tolstoy's pages. He and Sonya discussed them all. Not only was Natasha, the quicksilver heroine, based on a real person; traits of Tolstoy himself can be found in proud, moody Prince Andrey and in gentle, awkward Pierre, the open-minded searcher who sifts life, asking, "What is good? What is bad?" The character of Prince Bolkonsky was drawn from Tolstoy's stern Grandfather Volkonsky, and Count Rostov from grandfather Tolstoy, the extravagant governor of Kazan; and the fictional Sonya from Aunt Tatyana. Princess Maria, quiet, genuine, and plain, represents the personality of Tolstoy's mother.

Sonya was delighted with his project. When her husband was filled with the excitement of creation, her world became purposeful, interesting, important. She happily agreed to help copy the manuscript by hand.

Several chapters were already down on paper when an accident occurred. One afternoon Tolstoy mounted his favorite horse, Mashka. Taking along the silky white wolfhounds, Lubka and Krylat, he was soon galloping over the snowy landscape. The swift borzois ducked their narrow heads and raced away as they picked up the scent of a hare. But when the lone hunter tried to leap a narrow ravine, he was thrown so hard he plunged into unconsciousness. It seemed hours before he came to. Affectionate Krylat was licking his face. Lubka shivered nervously nearby. The horse had disappeared.

As his head began to clear, a strange thought occurred to Tolstoy. "I am a writer!" Then the heavy pain of a broken right arm overwhelmed him. Dragging himself to a nearby road, he prayed that someone would come before dark. At last a peasant found him. Late that night, Sonya hurried to the dingy little hut where her husband lay on a cot. His damp, twisted face looked white in the smoky glare of an oil lamp. Sonya could hardly breathe in the stifling hut; she was far along in her second pregnancy. She asked the peasants to lift Tolstoy into a cart and take him home.

A doctor from Tula managed to set the broken arm, but it did not heal. Six weeks later Tolstoy went to consult doctors in Moscow. Sonya made the sign of the cross as his carriage rolled down the drive. A daughter, Tanya, had just been born, and young Sergei was ill with smallpox, so she could not accompany her husband.

A room at the Behrses' Moscow home was prepared for surgery. Chloroform fumes filled every corner of the apartment. Tolstoy's bones were wrenched apart again by two strong men, then surgeons worked for hours resetting the break. Impatient at the idleness of his recuperation period, Tolstoy persuaded Tanya and Lisa to take dictation. He was full of ideas and dialogues for the new book. The girls would scribble happily for hours, sighing when he exclaimed, "No, a cliché won't do," or "Strike that out."

Before leaving Moscow he was asked to read from the new novel at a party. Here was a chance to trot out his beloved characters like talented children performing before company. He could not resist. In the friends' gracious drawing room a lamp flickered over his bandaged arm and pale face. He began reading hesitantly. But soon he sensed his listeners' interest, and his deep, resonant voice grew stronger and more varied, as the creatures of his brain—Pierre, the Bolkonskys, the Rostovs, and others— made their debuts. The small audience had heard that Tolstoy's characters were modeled after friends and members of his family. Everyone was busy guessing which real person had posed unwittingly for which role. When fictional Natasha made her entrance, a friend of Tanya's winked. The reading ended and everyone talked at once while tea was served. Guests praised the work extravagantly. Old Dr. Behrs basked in his son-in-law's reflected glory. The tired author smiled, but said little. He missed Sonya.

Tolstoy was happy to return to his family and he felt energetic enough to stage a fantastic Twelfth Night costume ball. Peasant musicians, garlands of greenery, outlandish disguises, dancing, and fireworks reminded many guests of the old days at Yasnaya. Holding a bandura awkwardly with his bad arm, the jovial host strummed Christmas carols while everyone sang. The evening's revelry was later written into the new novel as the Christmas celebration at the Rostovs'.

The work on his epic seemed to transform every facet of Tolstoy's life. In a reply to Fet's compliments of Sonya, he wrote gaily, "I'm glad you like my wife. Though I love her less than my novel, she's my wife, you know, all the same." But in his diary he rejoiced, "My relationship with Sonya has grown stronger and steadier," and also, "Not one person in a million, I dare say, is as happy as we are together." His occasional doldrums had evidently disappeared.

He arranged to publish the novel serially in Katkov's *Russian Herald*. Katkov was paying almost six times as much per sheet as *Boyhood* and *Youth* had brought. According to custom, groups of chapters would be published as soon as they were finished, long before the end of the book was fully planned. In February the first twenty-eight chapters came out. This was background material, in which the introduction of characters was just begun. Though public response was less than enthusiastic, nothing deterred the ambitious author from his plan.

During the winters Tolstoy frequently went to Moscow to continue his historical research in archives and libraries. One day, reading an eyewitness account of the War of 1812, he crowed with scholarly pleasure in his diary:

> I read with delight the history of Napoleon and Alexander. At once I was enveloped in a cloud of joy . . . of the possibility of doing . . . a psychological novel of Alexander and Napoleon, . . . of all the baseness, empty words, folly, all the contradictions of these men and of the people surrounding them.

He would also show how these posturing "great men" were themselves the pawns of circumstance and destiny.

Sometimes the whole Tolstoy family moved to Moscow for the season, but usually Sonya stayed behind at Yasnaya with the children. In many loving letters Tolstoy appeased her loneliness. "I always love you more when I'm parted from you. . . ." he wrote. "My soul, my darling, the best in the world! For God's sake, do not fail to write me every day. . . ." The wife at home showed young Sergei his absent father's picture, and the child exclaimed, "Papa! I love you terribly!" In 1866 another boy, Ilya, had been born, and Sonya complained to her sister, "I keep weaning or nursing or washing or boiling and apart from that there are the children, the pickling, the jam-making, the . . . copying. . . ." Of all her duties she liked best copying the great novel. If only he would leave it as he first wrote it down, without so many corrections! But Tolstoy was constantly crossing out, rearranging, and improving his work. Some portions of the story Sonya recopied by hand twenty times, but she was intensely proud of the results. Mailing off a batch of the manuscript to her husband, she commented:

> As I send off this package of paper to Moscow, I feel I am abandoning a baby to the elements; I'm afraid something may happen to it. I like what you are writing very much. I do not think I shall care as much for any other book of yours as this one.

At first the novel was called *The Year 1805*. Tolstoy soon changed the title to *All's Well That Ends Well*. Then one day he found a better name. His thoughts had wandered back to 1861, when he had visited with the writer Proudhon in Brussels. Proudhon had shown a tract entitled *War and Peace*. What a noble name for an epic. It was in excellent taste to borrow a title. So it was decided that the novel would be called *War and Peace*.

By 1867 Tolstoy was totally immersed in the work, often writing until he was dizzy and his head ached. His young wife managed the estate, saw to the three children, and carefully shielded her husband from distractions. In March he attended the funeral of Dyakov's wife. Soon another message came from Granny telling of her sister's death. Death, death. Dmitri, Nicholas. Now these friends. Perhaps he would die without finishing this task before him. He felt despair. How could one expect to write an epic about life in the face of death? He became depressed and nervous, but he continued the punishing hours at his writing table.

In a letter to a friend about this time, he tried to spell out the nature of a strange woe he felt:

> I shall soon be forty—I have loved truth more than anything; I do not despair of finding it, and I am still searching and searching. . . . But I'm alone, and it is hard and terrible, and it seems that I have lost my way.

One day Tolstoy bellowed at Sonya for no reason at all, and hurled a tray of teacups to the floor in an unprecedented temper tantrum. "Why?" gasped Sonya, more astonished than resentful, "What have I done?"

"Get out! Get out!" he shouted. He snatched a thermometer from its hook and smashed it against the wall. Shaken, he himself could not explain exactly what had happened. Sonya was afraid. When he was calm again he agreed to go to Moscow and consult a specialist.

The trip to the city was necessary for business purposes also. That summer the second part of *War and Peace* had come out, and public response was again mediocre. On Sonya's advice, the author decided to discontinue publishing serially, and to wait to print the book in six bound volumes as his own business venture. Bartenyev, a new publisher, would get ten per cent of the selling price and the printer would take twenty per cent. Tolstoy was advancing the capital and would earn seventy per cent of the profits. If the book were successful, he stood to gain a great deal. A medical specialist examined him and suggested that perhaps his nerves were strained, but Tolstoy refused any kind of treatment. He was cheerful, in fact, delighted with his publishing venture. He felt completely himself again.

The story of *War and Peace* is fiction, but the War of 1812 that inspired the fiction was real. Tolstoy was anxious to make every historical detail as accurate as possible. He decided to visit the battleground at Borodino. Here, in a turning point of the war, the Russian army had clashed violently with Napoleon's forces. Tolstoy borrowed an old hunting cart and took along Sonya's twelve-year-old brother, Stepan, for company. The boy was thrilled to be traveling with his interesting brother-in-law, dredging up memories of old heroes. Tolstoy himself was so excited that he forgot the box lunch Dr. Behrs had ordered for them.

The village of Borodino lay about seventy miles southwest of Moscow. When they arrived, a September drizzle was soaking the two-mile stretch of plain which had comprised the old battle lines. Guided by an old peasant and by military maps he had brought along, Tolstoy eagerly identified the places, the plan and the action that had begun on August 26, 1812, at six in the misty morning. The cart rattled over rocky ground as Tolstoy pointed out landmarks. Huskily he recounted the losses in the battle: 42,000 Russian soldiers and twenty-two general officers. Napoleon had lost one-fourth of his army and thirty-one generals.

That night the author wrote his wife from a convent inn: "I'm very, very satisfied with my trip. If God gives me health and peace of mind, I'll write such a description of the Battle of Borodino as was never written before."

By December of that year, he had completed three volumes, about half the novel. To increase the plausibility of the story, he sprinkled the crowds of characters with real people: Napoleon, fat and nervous, sitting his horse poorly, a strange little man who found a thrill in gazing at dead and wounded Russian soldiers; Tsar Alexander I, proud and stubborn; the shrewd and sluggish Russian General Kutuzov, and others.

The three completed volumes of *War and Peace* were printed and sent out to Moscow bookstores. Tolstoy was staying with the Behrses, who were all very interested in his book. Early on the morning that the critics' reviews were to come out in the newspapers, he rose, dressed, and paced about, unwilling to leave the house before he had the critics' evaluations of his work.

With few exceptions, the first volumes of *War and Peace* were overwhelmingly praised.

During the next two years Tolstoy labored over the rest of his vast story. Dr. Behrs died. Another son, Leo, was born to the Tolstoys. The writer wept and rejoiced, then pushed ahead with his project. Finally, he struggled to conclude the epilogue and the last trifling corrections. An epic emerged.

The public response was enormous and enthusiastic. Literate Russia evidently raced to the bookstores to snatch up every copy of *War and Peace*. Those who could not buy it managed to borrow it, volume by volume. Young people identified themselves flatteringly with Natasha, Prince Andrey, or Pierre. Old men saw themselves as General Kutuzov. Elderly women relished the love stories. All cheered again the great conquest over Napoleon. *War and Peace* made them proud to be Russian—a people, as Tolstoy put it, essentially spiritual and courageous.

It soon became evident that foreigners were also appreciating the novel. Then Tolstoy was applauded again in his own country as the first Russian author to tell the world, See what a fine, fascinating race we Russians are, and what a great land is ours.

But foreigners were saying, This book is not only about Russia. It is about people, and people are the same the world over. *War and Peace* may be another *Odyssey* or *Iliad*.

Tolstoy had found his epic. But the author did not rejoice for long. The next ten years of his life were marked by a growing but unnamed depression which often plunged him into despair and finally threatened his life.

DESPAIR

The image in the mirror was entirely familiar: ordinary face, full beard, aristocratic bearing; a muscular man dressed in the dark wool smock of a peasant. But in those eyes was terrible desperation. "Why do I live?" Tolstoy inquired of his face in the glass. The voice was his, but how it choked with anxiety. Then the room was silent. Or was someone laughing softly? Was God amused? Was there a God?

"Why do I live?" Silence. It seemed there was no answer. This question, issuing from the depths of Tolstoy's soul, would recur with virulent frequency during the sixth decade of his life.

By the world's standards, Tolstoy was at forty-eight a most fortunate man. He himself acknowledged that outwardly he had achieved much in the way of family happiness, wealth, and intellectual accomplishments. He was blessed by good health. His name was internationally known, and he was praised everywhere for his writings. Earnings from *War and Peace*, the tremendously successful epic, amounted to many thousands of rubles a year. *Anna Karenina*, a contemporary novel, was just now being corrected and finished. It was already sold to a publisher, and the public was eager to read it. The Tolstoy estates, Nikolskoye (which Leo had inherited from Nicholas) and Yasnaya Polyana, were constantly improving and producing cattle, horses, timber, and fine wheat crops. Altogether, his annual income at this time was worth about 30,000 rubles. In 1871 he had used earnings from his books to buy an estate of 6,750 acres in Samara, the primitive land of the steppe. His brother and his sons often accompanied him to check on the management of the new estate. Occasionally the entire family spent the summer there.

Sonya had seen to it that the Tolstoy style of life was one to be envied. The house at Yasnaya had been enlarged and remodeled. The central structure, which Tolstoy had sold in 1854, had been handsomely replaced. There was plenty of room for the endless stream of guests on extended visits. Extra servants in crimson waistcoats appeared among the regular retainers.

In the first ten years of their marriage, six children were born to Tolstoy and Sonya: two girls, Tanya and Masha; and four boys, Sergei, Ilya, Leo, and Petya. "All happy families resemble one another," Tolstoy declared in the novel *Anna Karenina*. Yet the group at Yasnaya Polyana seemed unique in many ways. Into a box on the stair landing, children, parents, and guests would slip jokes, comic verse, and anonymous notes, to be read with glee at the large dinner table. The whole family kept diaries, played piano duets, picked mushrooms, went sleigh-riding, looked over illustrations for *War and Peace*, put on plays, read perpetually, and organized costume balls. Tolstoy played football with the boys. In the summers they swam in the river or went fishing. The children took turns at the chessboard and at riding the donkeys, Bismarck and McMahon. Tolstoy had developed a passion for astronomy, and warm evenings might be spent examining the sky. Frequently the family visited neighboring estates. There were tremendous dinners, music and dancing—quadrilles, polkas, and waltzes. Chefs turned out colorful fruit ices and unbelievable dishes, such as cottages made of waffles, served with cream sauce.

The young Tolstoys admired and loved their famous father. When the black despair was upon him, they respected and feared his unhappiness. But when his mood was frivolous and playful, everyone's spirits brightened. The young ones cried with pleasure

in his strong grasp, breathing the smell of his peasant blouse. The older children found him the jolliest of companions. No guessing game could outwit him. "Ah, what a Papa ours is!" they marveled. Under his direction, clearing the snow from the pond for a skating party could be more fun than the skating itself. Together they read *Around the World in Eighty Days* and *The Three Musketeers* aloud in French. Tolstoy prudently omitted passages he considered unfit for children.

Sometimes company visiting on a winter day would seem interminably dull. After such guests left, the children watched their father for a traditional nonsense signal. Sitting in his armchair, the sober host would slowly raise one arm, one finger high in the air. Then with a sidelong glance he would murmur, "Numidian cavalry?" As he jumped up lightly and raced around the house in a ludicrous canter, his "cavalry" clattered after him, waving, shouting, working off steam. Around and around over the polished parquet floors they paraded. All resentments and boredom were cured in the charge of the Numidians.

Among other games was the passing fad of telling fortunes with cards. The first time Tanya tried it, she laid out a hand entirely composed of spades. She called her mother to come and tell her what the hand meant. Sonya looked over the child's shoulder and caught her breath. She told Tanya in a frightened voice that the cards said an old man would die while traveling. The girl put the incident into her diary, commenting, "Nonsense! Rubbish! I refuse to believe it."

Among the guests of the Tolstoys were famous authors. In 1878 Tolstoy wrote to make amends with Turgenev. The two men had not seen each other since a dispute seventeen years earlier. The aging author came to visit again at Yasnaya Polyana. He intrigued the family with tales of Parisian life. One night the cancan was mentioned. The children watched the tall, elegant guest. "The old cancan is a proper and graceful dance," he said slyly, looking around at his audience. "There was a time when I could dance it. Perhaps I might even dance it now." To Tolstoy's embarrassment, Turgenev slipped out of his chair, thrust his thumbs into his waistcoat armholes, and began to kick and dance. The show was irresistible. Sonya and the children were delighted. Finally, as the comical gentleman progressed in his wild, suggestive prancing, their gloomy host also joined in the laughter. Another time, returning from a walk and some serious conversation, Tolstoy and his visitor climbed onto a seesaw the boys had built. Soon two brilliant minds and bearded countenances were gliding gently up and down, to the joy of the children. They eyed each other sheepishly across the board. Surely the quarrel was patched up at last.

In the winter when fewer guests visited Yasnaya Polyana, the big house was still crowded with children, servants, two governesses, and a tutor. Their father had started the young ones off in their studies, instructing them in math. Sonya helped to teach them Russian. More tutors moved in: Mlle. Gachet, whom Tanya claimed for her own; Annie for Masha, the younger sister; and B. A. Alexeyev, the language teacher, with his family of three. Other instructors came in for drawing lessons, music, Greek, and German.

The children's relationship with their father was generally a firm bond. As Tanya remarked to her diary, "When you talk to him everything becomes so clear. . . ." She could not realize how he longed to make things clear for himself.

"Why do I live? . . . What is the meaning of my life?" he often wondered.

Although he had begun to fear that he was drifting into madness, Tolstoy still worked with the vigor of a plow horse. In addition to supervising the estates, he was finishing *Anna Karenina* and polishing a simple, attractive *Reader* for the peasants; it included stories of his dog Boulka, fables, and folk tales. Four more such primers were to follow. The first one sold nearly a million copies—to the astonishment of its writer.

Almost as surprising to him was the success of *Anna Karenina*. About the time that these were published he was directing seventy new schools in his district. However, he seemed to care less and less for teaching or for writing. In a letter to a friend he said, "Perhaps . . . I shall never write another word!"

Sonya was constantly aware that some dreadful obsession held her husband. "His lack of direction is a great trial to him," she lamented in her diary. "Sometimes he thinks he is losing his mind, and his fear of insanity is so intense that I am terrified when he tells me about it afterward."

Occasionally the memory of a journey he had taken several years earlier would surge through his mind. When had it been? Yes, just after *War and Peace* was completed. In 1869. Where had he been going? To the province of Penza, to buy land. It seemed then that the answer to life lay in securing wealth, in owning more farms, in producing more crops on acres and acres, all his own. The trip had started happily. A young servant, Sergei Arbuzov, had gone with him. The two had laughed together at the squeal of the big train engine, the sights and sounds of the passengers, and the excitement of traveling through the autumn air. From Nizhni Novgorod they proceeded by horse-drawn hired coach. The boy talked on, but an unusual feeling of dread had come upon Tolstoy. He decided to spend the night in Arzamas. They found the old town dark and silent. The inn-keeper, who had a hideous spot on one cheek, showed them to the only room he had. It was painted white with wine-colored doors and woodwork. Sergei unpacked the samovar and began to prepare tea, but Tolstoy fell asleep on the dirty divan of imitation leather, too weary to drink from the steaming glass. When he woke in the strange room, the stale blackness seemed overpowering. Terror seized him. "Why have I come here?" he said aloud. ". . . Here I am, the whole of me! . . . Why am I depressed? What am I afraid of?"

"Me!" It seemed that Death itself was answering him. "I am here!" said Death.

Tolstoy lay shuddering with nausea in the forbidding dark. He knew that Death was at work. He lighted the stump of a candle. The flickering, reddish flame caught at last, casting shadows around the dark room. He tried to think of his warm, cheerful country home, his family, now dearer than ever. It struck him that he could hardly remember their faces. "Nothing exists but death," his voice sounded, desperate, "and death should not be!" He made an effort to pray, but a menacing presence seemed near. "Sergei!" he shouted at last, rushing into the hall. He woke the boy and told him to get the horses harnessed. They must leave immediately. The startled servant ran out to the stables.

104

When he returned, he found his master sleeping soundly on the couch. The nightmare was past. Sergei let him rest. This chilling experience at Arzamas returned to haunt Tolstoy many times. Did it mean that Death was beside him?

And a season appeared when death did seem to stalk the Tolstoy family. One day Tolstoy made his usual visit to failing Aunt Tatyana in her upstairs room. She called him "Nicholas," his father's name, and asked that he take her and her belongings to a downstairs bedroom. Faintly she said, "I'll move there so as not to spoil your nice top room by dying in it." He remonstrated that she would soon be well and strong again. But she insisted. So he had her silver icon, her jars from the dresser, and chests of dark clothing taken to the paneled lower bedroom. Her tired eyes looked fondly at him.

Auntie died on June 20, 1874, but by then another loss had already left the family numb with grief. The baby, Petya, died when he was a year old. Sonya was inconsolable: "He died . . . after only two days' illness. . . . My darling, I loved him so much, and now everything seems so empty since they buried him yesterday. My mind refuses to take in that my Petya and the dead baby are one and the same. . . ." Tolstoy wept helplessly. Six months later Sonya bore another boy. They named him Nicholas. This child lived not quite a year. In 1875 came a daughter, Vavara. She stopped breathing a few minutes after birth. That was in October.

Old Aunt Pelagya, Tolstoy's sociable guardian from Kazan, had moved in with the family when Tatyana died. She was pleased to be at Yasnaya again, and immediately started giving orders to everyone. But only a few months later, she too sickened, and in December, 1875, she passed away. Sonya and Tolstoy wondered if they could take any more death. Exhausted, Sonya tried to be brave for her husband's sake, but she was mourning not only her dead babies. It seemed she was losing her husband as well, for something more than grief was plaguing him. "Why is he punishing me?" she puzzled.

Questions bombarded Tolstoy's weary spirit. "Why should I live, why wish for anything or do anything?" And to these questions he wearily replied, "I do not know." He turned to the philosophers for help—to Socrates, Arthur Schopenhauer, King Solomon, and others. But their answers seemed only to lead to further depressing questions. "The wise man seeks death all his life and therefore death is not terrible to him," said Socrates. And Solomon wrote, "For the living know that they shall die: but the dead know not any thing. . . . Their love, and their hatred, and their envy, is now perished. . . ." Schopenhauer seemed to erase hope even in the present, saying, "This so real world of ours with all its suns and milky way is nothing." During this dismal time Tolstoy grieved often for his family. Loving them, he shuddered to think that he could not hide the terrible truth from them. "And the truth is death."

It came to him that there were four possible paths out of this dilemma. The first was blithe ignorance. Not knowing that life is hopeless would mean not caring. It was too late for that. The second was the way of pleasure. Just eat, drink, and be merry, as Solomon suggested. Most people followed this path, but Tolstoy could not. The third escape was strong and energetic. If life is evil, then it must be destroyed. Suicide? Could he come to that? Perhaps. He found himself feebly following the fourth way—the despicable path of weakness. Clinging to his life weakly, he was almost certain that it had no purpose, nor any meaning which could not be destroyed by death.

One night Tolstoy sat very late in his study, the vaulted room on the first floor. As usual, he was brooding about how evil life can be. He noticed a strong cord, probably left on the couch by one of the boys. He looked up. The stout supports which divided the room would hold up his weight if he hanged himself by that cord. Since life is evil, should it not be destroyed? He buried his face in his hands, appalled by his horrible thoughts. Quickly he put away the cord. Then he seized his hunting guns and hid these out of his sight. It was true that he feared life; still he hoped, he hoped for something. He blew out the lamp on the writing table and started upstairs to bed, feeling for the balustrade of the staircase as he did each night. In the room above, his wife was suddenly wakened by a hoarse cry in the darkness, "Sonya! Sonya!"

She lit a candle and rushed out in her nightgown to find him wandering along the hall. "What happened, Lyovotchka?"

106

"Nothing," he mumbled in embarrassment. "I lost my way." Rescued from a terror that had overcome him, he followed her humbly to their room.

Safe in his bed, however, he tossed restlessly, remembering an old Eastern fable. Was he dreaming? It seemed that he traveled through a vast desert and then fell down, down, into a deep well. Struggling to save himself, he managed to grasp a green twig which grew on the steep side of the well. He clung to this little branch. Looking below, he saw a fearsome dragon opening huge jaws to devour him if he fell further. His hands were weakening. He was pale with fright. Still he gripped the twig. Two mice appeared, a black and a white one, and began to gnaw the leafy stem he was grasping. Soon, it seemed, the twig would be nibbled away, and he would fall into the dragon's jaws. Then, strangely, he noticed a few drops of oozing honey on the remaining leaves. Instinctively, he reached with his tongue for the consolation of the honey. He woke and sat up in bed perspiring. "The two drops of honey . . . my love of family and of writing. . . ." he said aloud. And the black and white mice were night and day greedily gobbling up the twig of time. He saw the dragon plainly, and the honey was no longer sweet in his mouth. The dragon of Death seemed inescapable.

Did God know of his suffering struggles? Was there a God? Sometimes he felt these strange questionings had gone on within him forever, through childhood, in the Caucasus, at Sevastopol, at home and abroad, all his life. He recalled a long-ago afternoon when a friend had proudly announced to him and his brothers that it had been discovered at school that there is no God. Tolstoy tried to remember what his own belief had been then. "I believed in a God," he said, "or rather I did not deny God. . . . Neither did I deny Christ and his teaching, but what his teaching consisted in, I again could not have said. . . ." Then he realized in disgust that his only real faith all his life had been a belief in perfecting himself. And he honestly, humbly tried from that moment to seek a relationship to God, not once or twice, but dozens of times. Yet often he would end by saying sadly to himself that God did not exist.

"My heart was oppressed with a painful feeling," he wrote

later in *A Confession*, "which I can only describe as a search for God. . . . That search for God was not reasoning . . . not from the course of my thoughts . . . but proceeded from the heart." One day, walking through an early spring forest, listening to the birds and looking at the twisted leaves of new green, from old habit he began to pray. And despairing that there was no God, he shouted into the stillness of the wood, "Lord, have mercy, save me!" The distraught questioner became suddenly, gloriously aware that a compassionate Someone understood his struggling search.

"He exists," Tolstoy exclaimed with joy. And the instant that he admitted God's existence, new life welled up within him.

"What more do you seek?" asked a small voice. "This is He. He is that without which one cannot live. . . . Live seeking God and then you will not live without God." And the searcher was saved. And he began to live again.

GROWING FAITH

Faith in God is the meaning of life! Why had Tolstoy not seen it before? "I live, really live, only when I feel Him and seek Him," he wrote. His striving for self-perfection, his attempts to teach the peasants were matters of vanity. "I could not teach anything needful for I did not know what was needful." His earlier years now seemed pretentious; the struggle for fame and money was a selfish absurdity. For a long time his mind had played a cruel trick on him. Now he was determined to lead a godly life.

The thinker humbled himself and tried to return to the rites and rituals of the Orthodox Church, the faith of his father. Sonya rejoiced. He received communion, fasted, prayed the set prayers, genuflected—conformed. It felt so good to abase himself. But again and again his reason rebelled. He felt that much of the service was artificial and false to the point of blasphemy. "Vanquish the enemy" was a constant prayer, since Russia was then at war with Turkey. "A Christian should pray for his enemies, not against them," agonized the convert. He remembered the terrible siege of Sevastopol, seeing robed priests holding up their crucifixes, urging bloody men to fight to the death. It became hideously apparent to Tolstoy that mass murders had often been carried on in the name of Christ. What was the true faith? What was falsehood? To find the reality of Christ's teachings he turned away from the Orthodox Church to an urgent study of the New Testament. Russia's greatest novelist decided to give up writing fiction.

He would now inform the world of his findings in the Gospels. Great artistic expressions of his faith in God, along with original ideas for following the precepts of Christ, began to come from his pen. He discovered the Sermon on the Mount as if its ideas were brand new, then he zealously tried to apply it to the life around him. Always he praised the simple goodness of the peasants, as he brashly rebuked the government's stranglehold on their lives. He began to deplore the Church's deference to the State rather than to the teachings of Christ. He proclaimed that the Church was a partner of the State, "cheating and fleecing the people." Tolstoy's new philosophical writing was censored, confiscated, and suppressed by the Tsar's angry officials. Nevertheless, copies kept circulating and were read and reverenced by thousands. But Sonya and several of Tolstoy's children bitterly rejected his new thoughts. The people's extravagant adoration, the government's attempts to restrain his vigorous writings, and his family's lack of understanding were to form the pattern for Tolstoy's last thirty years.

The doctrine of nonviolence was rapidly taking root in his mind. As he constantly pondered the Gospels in the light of his religious experience, it seemed to Tolstoy that all violence was immoral. Why could mankind not search for and find peace? He felt that the heart of the Gospels was in Matthew 5:39. How strange that it had so often been overlooked. When Christ said, "Resist not evil," he simply meant not to use violence *anywhere* for *any* purpose! From the Sermon on the Mount Tolstoy drew several principles which formed his doctrine of nonresistance. He recorded them later in a long essay called *What I Believe*:

> (1) Christ bids us not be angry with anyone. . . .
> Live at peace with all men and never consider
> your anger against any man justified.
> (2) Never resist the evildoer by force, do not meet

violence with violence. If they beat you, endure it; if they take your possessions, yield them up; if they compel you to work, work. . . .

(3) Do not consider the people of other nations to be enemies, but account all men as brothers. . . . Love them and do good to them. Men need only trust Christ's teaching and obey it and there will be peace on earth. . . .

It was so simple.

As Tolstoy's religious writings and personality became increasingly admired by the masses, his family, and especially his wife, reacted with growing dislike. Conservative Sonya was horrified that her husband's zeal for religion could lead him to repudiate the Orthodox Church. She was sure she could never waver in her church allegiance. "Not one stone can be removed from the holy edifice without destroying the harmony of the whole," she declared. In 1879 she wrote to her sister:

> Leo is still working! . . . He reads and thinks until it gives him a headache. And all in order to prove that the Church does not accord with the Gospels. There are not ten people in Russia who can be interested in such a subject. . . . My only hope is that he will soon get over it, and it will pass, like a disease.

When he was not writing his new, didactic pieces, Tolstoy frequently farmed in the fields with the peasants he admired. Dressed in a rough homespun blouse and bark slippers, he lustily sang a folk song as he swung a heavy blade, gathering the golden hay. His forehead glistened with sweat in the summer sun. Each day he exerted himself in some such manual labor, plowing, haying, sawing wood, or making clumsy shoes at a cobbler's bench. All this was a part of his new philosophy. He urged his children to join in these projects, but their enthusiasm usually did not equal his.

On a spring afternoon in March of 1881, Tolstoy was striding

112

along the highway near his home, getting some exercise after a rain. A wandering beggar came toward him. In his hand the young man carried a bird in a cage. The middle-aged hiker who looked like a peasant spoke pleasantly to the boy, "Where from? Where to?"

The boy answered brokenly. "From Tula, bad business, I had no food, my bird has not eaten, they killed the Tsar."

Tolstoy stopped astonished. "What Tsar? Who killed him? When?"

"The Russian Tsar, St. Petersburg, threw a bomb. . . ." Incredulous, Tolstoy returned to the house and sent to Tula for the papers, to learn the details of the assassination.

In St. Petersburg a young revolutionary had thrown a bomb at the carriage of Tsar Alexander II as he rode in the street beside the Katerina Canal. The horses were killed and two members of his guard were wounded, but the ruler had escaped injury. Instead of leaving the scene, the Tsar stopped to question his assailant, who had been seized. Then a second bomb was thrown by another conspirator lurking in the crowd. This explosion crushed the body of the Emperor; he fell in the snow at the feet of his first attacker. The stunned royal escort carried him to the Winter Palace nearby, where, several hours later, he died. The assassin and five other revolutionaries, including one woman, were arrested. Six times before, this group of plotters had attempted to murder the Tsar. Quietly jubilant over their success, they were herded off to prison.

These revolutionaries may have feared that if the masses became united under Alexander II, the general revolution they hoped for would be averted. Certainly this Tsar had done more for the common people of Russia than any other ruler. It was he who had liberated the serfs in 1861. He had helped negotiate the treaty following the disastrous Crimean War. On the very day of his murder he had approved a plan for the beginnings of representative government, laying the groundwork for a constitution which would at last grant the peasants a political voice.

At Yasnaya, Tolstoy mourned over the murderous event and the death of a great man. Perhaps he remembered his own early introductions to violence. Christ crucified, hanging on Aunt

Tatyana's wall ("Auntie, why did they torture Him?"); Prosper de St. Thomas, the tutor, threatening young Leo and locking him in a closet; Kuzma the groom dragged off to the barn for a beating; the shattering siege of Sevastopol—the dead, the dying, the mutilated men. Probably the most gruesome of such memories was the guillotining he had witnessed so long ago in Paris. The white neck of the prisoner bent beneath the gleaming blade. The hush of the huge crowd. The sound of the knife. The loud thump of the bloody severed head dropping into the box. Tolstoy groaned, "Do not execute; the more you execute, the more evil there will be. . . . Do not execute, evil cannot be cut off by evil."

In his mind's eye Tolstoy saw the maimed body of the Tsar lying in a pool of blood on the snowy St. Petersburg street. He was haunted also by a brutal vision of the death that awaited the killers. Lying down to nap on the black leather sofa in his study, he dreamed: The six assassins of the Tsar stood for sentencing by a black-robed judge. But wait. The judge's beard, his eyes, his face—Tolstoy's own face! The prisoners gazed stoically ahead as they were condemned. Then each was revealed as a replica of himself, the dreamer. And the sneering hangman standing ready with a rope was another Leo Tolstoy! He awoke gasping. He decided to petition the new Tsar, Alexander III, asking him to pardon his father's murderers.

At morning coffee the next day he discussed the matter with his children's tutor, Alexeyev, a bright young man who respected him profoundly. Tolstoy felt that in spite of their violent methods, the revolutionaries' ideals were lofty: universal well-being, equality, and liberty. He had decided that condemning a few of them to death would be useless. Some ideal greater than theirs must be found. A tremendous act of love and forgiveness, such as pardoning the assassins, might touch the masses and deter them from revolution and violence. He told the tutor that he was going to beg the new Tsar to forgive them. The tutor approved the bold plan. Such a great act of forgiveness by the Tsar might save Russia.

Sonya heard their conversation and was shocked. "What are you saying!" she reproved the tutor. "Leo . . . does not need

114

your advice . . . !" Then she urged her husband to put aside his reckless idea. His inflammatory writings had already placed his family in danger. Husband and wife stared at each other. Their views were opposite, and between them there was very little understanding.

In spite of Sonya's scoldings, Tolstoy immediately drafted an appeal to the new ruler. As he wrote, he wept. The letter included this plea:

> It is . . . presumption and folly on my part to demand that you, the Emperor of Russia and a loving son, should pardon your father's murderers . . . returning good for evil. It is folly, yet I cannot do otherwise than wish it. . . .
>
> If you do not pardon, but execute the murderers, you will have done away with three or four individuals out of hundreds. . . . But forgive, return good for evil, and . . . thousands, millions of your subjects will thrill with joy and affection at this act of mercy from a throne. . . . Sire, if you did that, if you called these men before you, gave them some money and sent them away somewhere, to America, and wrote a manifesto beginning with the words, "But I say unto you, Love your enemies" . . . with what torrential force good and love would pour over Russia. . . . Then, as wax melts in the fire, the revolutionaries' opposition will melt in the deed of their Emperor, the man who fulfills the law of Christ.

Delivering such a letter into the hands of the Tsar was not easy. Tolstoy knew that administrative underlings might stifle such an entreaty, thinking it would disturb the Emperor. While the author's fame and influence were widespread now and becoming greater every year, he still had no prestige at court, unless one counted his aging cousin, Granny. At last he entrusted the petition to Strakhov, an old friend who knew one of the Emperor's favorite ministers. Strakhov admired Tolstoy's works and religious teachings, and felt honored by his mission. He approached the minister with Tolstoy's missive of peace. The minister read the letter and flatly refused to show it to the new Tsar.

Later, however, this minister worried that a copy of the letter might be circulated and might somehow come into the Tsar's hands. He drafted a letter telling the Tsar that there were some who would urge him to pardon the murderers, but that, as a Russian who lived among Russians, he knew that the people were eager for execution. A secretary read the minister's letter to the Emperor. Alexander III, a large, imposing man, turned cold gray eyes toward the secretary. "Be calm, . . ." he asserted metallically. "I guarantee that *all six will be hanged.*" Within a month the execution took place. Another opportunity had been lost to bring peace and unity to a divided and agitated Russia.

The new Tsar's administration soon proved harsher and more tyrannical than his father's. The press was rigidly controlled. Political discussion was strictly forbidden in public, and private dissent was usually kept very quiet. Unrest was everywhere, and many agreed with Tolstoy that the government's despotism would bring on more violence. And violence could only beget violence—it always had.

Tolstoy had almost stopped writing novels now, turning to religion and nonviolence. The family income had shrunk considerably. This disturbed Sonya, who was determined to bring up her children in luxury to continue the expensive aristocratic life that seemed normal to her. In 1885 Tolstoy reluctantly assigned to Sonya the reprinting rights to all of his books written before 1881, his best literary work. She immediately began to prosper in the publishing business. On the rest of his works, those published since 1881, Tolstoy put no restrictions, made no profits. They were his free gift to the people of Russia and the world. *A Confession*, published in Switzerland, described with beauty and honesty his search for God. Dozens of treatises established his ideas about the Gospels, the government, and the peasants. *The Death of Ivan Ilich* pleased Sonya because it was fiction, but this seventy-page short novel also crackles with the author's new thought in its realistic picture of a godless man dying. Tchaikovsky, whose music Tolstoy admired, said after reading *The Death* of *Ivan Ilich*, "I am convinced that the greatest author-painter who ever lived is Leo Tolstoy!" *The Kreutzer Sonata* shocked Russia. It is a powerful short novel revealing the immoral hate that can boil up within marriage. Gentler, simpler tales for the newly literate peasantry also appeared. A lengthy treatise called *The Kingdom of God Is Within You* demonstrates the futility of war, condemning munitions dealers, judges, generals, and the Orthodox Church as violence-mongers.

Between 1877 and 1889 Sonya bore five more children: Andrey, Michael, Alexis, Alexandra, and Ivan. Sonya and Leo had thirteen children in all. With each succeeding birth, Sonya became more exhausted and more reluctant to continue having children. She wrote to her sister, "I teach, and nurse like a machine from morn to night, from night to morn." Alexis and Ivan died in childhood, as had Petya, Nicholas, and Vavara years before. Alexandra, born in 1884 and nicknamed Sasha, later became her father's ardent disciple and his biographer. Sonya still copied Tolstoy's manuscripts, and rolled his cigarettes, although at last he did manage to give up smoking. She trimmed his beard when the moon was new, and catered to his off-and-on vegetarian diet. But she could not share his unusual faith. Her loyalty remained with the rituals and traditions of the Russian Orthodox Church. When the family was in Moscow, she participated in a strenuous social life. At Yasnaya she continued her country duties. In both places she planned and presided at tremendous meals, as more and more visitors arrived to pay homage to the new religious leader, her husband. Tanya summed up one day's callers in her diary:

> Drunkards, long-haired nihilists, priests, and rich businessmen who would ask what to do with their money. . . . An officer came, and while he told his story sobbed so that we in the other room were all scared to death. Papa is nice to everybody who really needs his help or advice. . . .

By 1886 a steady stream of pilgrims flowed toward Yasnaya. Soon they were calling themselves "Tolstoyans." This term

117

came to identify those of Tolstoy's disciples who believed in nonviolence and deplored the oppression of the masses. An occasional group of Tolstoyans would give their possessions to the poor and live together following Christian principles. Such fellowships were established in Holland, the United States, and England in addition to those in Russia. Though Tolstoy reluctantly acknowledged himself as their leader, he actually deplored such "organizing." He had no wish to found a new sect. Nevertheless, there came to be Tolystoyans among peasants and students, upper-class Tolstoyans, and Tolstoyans among the foreign visitors who appeared almost daily on the doorstep of the estate. "How unattractive they all are, the followers, ..." Sonya complained. Two of the most dedicated disciples received Sonya's particular jealous scorn: Paul Biryukov, who became Tolstoy's biographer, and the handsome aristocrat Vladimir Chertkov, who was to be his editor. In spite of growing acclaim among the people, Tolstoy longed most of all for his own family's approval of his ideas, and their cooperation with his desire to live simply, in accordance with the Sermon on the Mount. But instead of agreeing with him or understanding him, for the most part they deplored the change in him—especially Sonya and the boys. Ilya complained:

> He often quarreled with Mama, and from the fun-loving, lively head of our family, he was transformed . . . into a stern, accusatory prophet. . . . We would be planning an amateur play, everybody was animated, chatting away, playing croquet, talking of love, etc. Papa appeared and with one word, or worse, with one look, everything was spoiled: The gaiety was gone. . . .

Though Sonya was pleased with the profits from publishing her husband's earlier novels, the family's rich, idle life (especially in Moscow) was an increasing shame to Tolstoy. He had decided that property was evil—the theft of the rich from the needy. He felt that his family's possessions and sumptuous ease were built on the backbreaking labor of the poor. "Jesus . . . bids us give up property, . . ." he remembered. But how could he ask his pampered brood to relinquish its carefree existence? Sometimes he longed to leave his family to their luxury and to end his days in solitude in a simple peasant's isba.

Meanwhile all Russia was discussing Tolstoy's philosophy. Sonya had said that not ten people in Russia would read his treatises, yet hundreds were so inspired by these writings on religion and nonresistance that they helped print and distribute them. The articles, published abroad or cranked out on hidden hand-turned printing presses, somehow found their way into many Russian homes. The people were hungry for freedom, and this strong, strange, unorthodox aristocrat, who looked like a peasant and wrote like one of the world's great artists, seemed to offer hope.

Sonya constantly urged her husband to stop his ranting against Church and State, war and the trappings of war. She knew that this would bring no money, and she feared it would bring trouble. Even Sergei, Tolstoy's usually tolerant brother, found he could not join in Tolstoy's religious zeal. Nor could Turgenev; from his deathbed in Paris he painfully scribbled a plea: "Dear friend, return to literature! That gift came to you from the same source as all the rest." But neither friends, family, Orthodox Church, nor the Tsar's censors could stop the treatises on nonviolence that poured from Tolstoy's heart. Nor could his confident search for peace be quelled. As the handprinted copies of his forbidden works inflamed and stirred the common people of Russia, he became a hero, a "prophet" to thousands.

THE DOCTRINE OF NONVIOLENCE

In 1891 drought scorched the provinces of central Russia and created a devastating famine. While the government callously ignored the disaster, hundreds of peasants were slowly dying of starvation in Ryazan and other provinces. In an impassioned appeal for help, the author Nicholai Leskov asked Tolstoy to alert Russia to the plight of her miserable, hungry people.

Tolstoy hesitated. He knew that one man could do little against so much wretchedness. In his reply to Leskov he postponed action with a lofty statement:

> To fight famine, all that is necessary is for men to do more good deeds. A good deed does not consist in giving bread to feed the famished, but in loving the famished as much as the overfed. Loving is more important than giving food. . . .

He mailed this theorizing letter, but questioned himself uneasily as to whether or not he should hurl himself into the struggle to feed the starving. He had repudiated the powerful established society. Could he now beg it for a pittance for the poor? In his dining room Sonya's cooks produced the usual ample array of appetizing dishes. The aroma of delicious food filled the air. There was no famine at Yasnaya Polyana. Sleep evaded the master of the house that night.

Against Sonya's wishes, he left two days later for a tour of the drought areas, taking with him his older daughters, Tanya and Masha. They were appalled by what they found. Everywhere the large sad eyes of listless, bony children stared at them over swollen, empty bellies. Gaunt peasant mothers deprived themselves of their little food in order to keep the young alive. Many had already died. Freezing peasants were burning roof thatch to warm their families, since they had no firewood, no heavy clothing, no furniture—nothing; all had been sold or bartered away for food.

Tolstoy hesitated no longer. This was no time for philosophizing about doctrines of love. These starving people needed his help. He could not remain aloof.

As he planned aid for the poverty-stricken, the author realized suddenly that he himself had no money. Six years before, he had turned over his most lucrative copyrights to his wife's publishing venture. Only recently he had publicly renounced the rights to his later works, making them common property. The announcement had been printed in most Russian newspapers on September 16, 1891: "I hereby grant to all who wish it the right to publish, without payment, in Russia and abroad . . . all the works written by me since the year 1881. . . ." Sonya had bitterly opposed this gift to the public. There were tears and reproaches. But at last she gave in, since she still held the rights to his earlier works. The estates had recently been divided among her and the nine children. Bickering had accompanied that decision also. Masha had refused her part, following her father's example of rejecting all ownership of property. The other children had promptly accused her of trickery, since her action forced them to face their own materialism. "Sorrow, sorrow, what weight, what torture!" moaned their father. But then how light and free he had felt after discarding the evil possessions! Only now he had no income of his own to share with the starving peasants.

His first unpleasant task was to ask his disapproving wife for money. He also had to tell her that he would be working in the provinces for months. Sonya was furious that he was deserting her for the entire winter. She gave him the money he asked, but accompanied it with a blistering retort. Then she took the four younger children and left for her usual pleasure season in Moscow.

Tanya and Masha went to work beside their famous father, who was now sixty-three years old. The drought had spread death across province after province. The extent of the need was shocking. They used Sonya's money to buy firewood, to set up crude bakeries, and to organize free kitchens. Almost fifteen hundred ragged skeletons crowded in twice a day to eat in the thirty kitchens opened that first month. Three months later, hundreds of kitchens had been organized, feeding ten thousand people daily. Tolstoy on horseback supervised volunteers and the distribution of supplies by day. By night, he composed a torrent of heartrending articles, pleading with Russia to help her perishing people. The articles were usually censored in Russia, but published abroad. At last money began to trickle in. Volunteers followed. Many of Tolstoy's articles laid the blame for the drastic food shortage squarely upon the shoulders of the nobility. In a story published in the *London Daily Telegraph* he said simply, "The people are starving because we eat too much. This has always been true, but this year's poor harvest has proved that the rope is stretched to breaking point. . . . The privileged classes . . . are guilty." Tolstoy seemed to be blaming the famine on the wealthy. In response to this accusation a rumble of displeasure spread through officialdom. An editorial in the *Moscow Gazette* exaggerated Tolstoy's ideas and increased the disquiet:

> Count Tolstoy's appeal is based on the most rabid,
> wild-eyed form of socialism. . . . He openly
> preaches social revolution. . . . He affirms that
> the rich subsist on the sweat of the people, con-
> suming everything they possess and produce.

Rumors spread that the writer who fed the poor might soon be forcibly confined to his estate, imprisoned in a monastery, or exiled.

In St. Petersburg one member of the privileged classes became very much alarmed by these rumors. Tolstoy's Granny, Alexandra Tolstoy, asked to speak to the Tsar. She received the kind reply that Alexandra III would call on her instead. When he appeared, Granny curtsied. Though fearful, she came right to the point. "In a few days a report will be made to you about shutting up in a monastery the greatest genius in Russia."

"Tolstoy?"

"You have guessed it, Sire," she replied in a soft voice.

"Does that mean he is plotting against my life?" asked the head of Church and State, with a sad smile, remembering the troublesome upstart's aversion to violence.

Granny gratefully returned his smile, for she knew by his tone that the Tsar would refuse harsh punishments for Tolstoy. She was right. Denying demands from others that the unusual Russian Count be taught a lesson, Tsar Alexander III told his ministers, "I ask you not to touch Tolstoy. I have no intention of making a martyr out of him and thus earning for myself universal indignation."

But somehow the administration had to quell this spreading concern for the starving. Newspapers were ordered to change the word "famine" to "failure of crops." The Tsar stated publicly, "In Russia there is no famine, but there are localities suffering from a failure of crops." Few were fooled. Most people realized that the government was ignoring its responsibility to the hungry and the poor. The exhausted author who was trying to help was acclaimed and admired.

In spite of their differences, Sonya and her husband corresponded almost daily whenever they were apart. To a lonely letter from her he replied, "I know only one thing, that I love you with all my soul, and I want to see you and calm you." His poignant descriptions of the needy brought tears to her eyes. In November she herself scratched out an urgent public plea for help. Her letter appeared in every Russian newspaper. It was translated and reprinted in Europe and America. To Sonya's amazement she soon had collected 13,000 rubles for the emergency. Tolstoy was joyous when he learned what she had done.

Through a freezing twilight in January of 1892, he returned wearily from his relief work to the old house in Ryazan where he was staying. A plump, familiar figure was waiting in the doorway. "Sonya!" he shouted and opened wide his arms. She breathed happily within his muscular embrace, saying she had come to work while Tanya kept their children in Moscow. For two weeks she visited soup kitchens and wretched, malodorous peasant huts. She stitched warm coats for emaciated children and put the account books in order. Then she returned to the city to continue her collections for the endless ranks of the hungry. Meanwhile their sons had joined the volunteers. Sergei and Ilya did what they could to bring relief in the province of Chern. Young Leo brought aid to Samara.

In 1892 another barren summer followed another dry springtime. Seedlings, so hopefully sown, soon shriveled brown. The resulting "poor harvest" filled no larders. Tolstoy and the little army of volunteers worked on. His famine articles attracted international attention. Inspired Americans sent seven boatloads of precious corn. Minnesota millers promised flour. All contributions of money were carefully budgeted to make them go as far as possible. But some peasants were afraid to come to the free kitchens. At the government's urging, priests in the stricken provinces were warning their people to stay away from the "Antichrist's" tables. Prodded by the priests, one fearful fellow asked:

> What kind of a Count is this, dressed in peasant fashion, going about the huts? . . . He's not a human being, he's Antichrist! Where does he get such power? He merely waves one arm—money pours down like rain! He waves the other—a cart with bread rolls right up to him! The bread he gives us comes from the devil . . . !

The devout peasants writhed under this pressure. But one answered gratefully, speaking of Tolstoy's daughters, "What

126

kind of Antichrist offspring are these?—they are God's angels, sent by the Lord." Neither Church nor State offered food for the thousands who were hungry. Only Tolstoy and his workers would help them keep the children alive until the next harvest.

In 1893 the rains returned. Crops prospered. The people were saved. Tolstoy came home.

The next year death overtook the Tsar who had ignored the famine and despair among his people. His handsome son immediately dashed any hope for a less oppressive regime. Nicholas II declared malevolently:

> I have heard that voices have recently been raised
> . . . of men carried away by the mad dream of
> electing representatives to participate in the in-
> ternal administration of the country. Let it be
> known to all that I . . . shall defend the principle
> of autocracy as unswervingly as did my late father.

This ruler was convinced that only a rigid government could ensure a safe nation. He could not know that he was to die a miserable death as Russia's last tsar. Following Alexander III's example, Nicholas II planned to keep a close watch on the world-famous writer loved by the people. But he warned his ministers not to touch Tolstoy, echoing his father: "I do not intend to add a martyr's crown to his glory." It was understood that the Tolstoyans, the followers, were to be persecuted.

At this time Tolstoy was writing an essay called "What Is Art?" Though he had said he would write no more fiction, he also began a short novel, *Hadji Murad*. His children were marrying. Old friends were dying. Visitors came constantly to hear his philosophy. From the United States came Jane Addams, the social worker. From Bohemia came Thomas Masaryk, a bold young professor who would become the first President of Czechoslovakia. Anton Chekhov and Maxim Gorky, important Russian writers, also visited. Artists Ilya Repin, Ivan Kramskoy, and Tolstoy's dear friend Nicholas Gay made their way to Yasnaya to paint the master's portrait. They were followed by unstable fanatics, salesmen, a criminologist, a psychologist, and, always, the perpetual parade of the poor.

Tolstoy was nearing seventy, but he still practiced gymnastics. He could work vigorously in the fields for three hours without stopping. He learned to ride a bicycle and took a childish pleasure in letting go of the handlebars as he rolled along. Twice during the last decade he had hiked the one hundred thirty miles from Moscow to Yasnaya, peasant style, with a pack on his back. When he joined the Temperance League, his daughter Tanya observed privately that her father really enjoyed denying himself. He insisted now on living very simply, keeping his own rooms cleaned, emptying his own chamber pots.

During the following years several religious groups appealed to Tolstoy for help against the atrocities of stern government authority. One of these sects, the Dukhobors, a large group of un-Orthodox Christians, had professed for over a hundred years the belief that military service and bearing arms was a sin; but they had occasionally defended themselves with pistols against plundering hill tribes in the Caucasus. In 1895, under the revival influence of a strong spiritual leader, thousands of the Dukhobors gathered in Tiflis to publicly burn their weapons, reaffirming their tenet of nonviolence. Government officials and the hierarchy of the State-controlled Orthodox Church were disturbed. They hated and feared this unusual Christian sect whose young men were now refusing to serve in the army. Drastic action was taken. A member of the Dukhobors described the weapon-burning incident to Tolstoy's son Sergei and he reported:

> They brought all their guns, daggers, revolvers, two cartfuls of coal, twenty carts of fuel and petrol. During the burning they prayed and sang psalms till two o'clock in the morning. . . . The Cossacks arrived with whips and began to flog . . . the people so mercilessly that you could not see the grass for blood. The Cossacks' leader could not disperse them, and they formed circles holding hands, to protect the womenfolk . . . while the governor himself helped to flog them. . . .

Thousands of the helpless Dukhobors were driven away into the mountains, where a great many died. Their homes were burned and their lands confiscated. Their leader had been banished.

When Tolstoy heard of this savagery, he covered his wrinkled face with his hands and wept. The old man began to try to relieve this sect of 7,000 gentle believers. He sent a vitriolic description of the outrageous mistreatment of the Dukhobors to London, where it was printed as *The Persecution of the Christians in Russia in 1895*. After that, Tolstoy and his followers Chertkov and Biryukov boldly published another article, in Russian, called "Give Help!" Copies went to every consequential member of the government, including Nicholas II. Instead of help, there came reprisal. The two devoted followers were exiled. Biryukov was deported to a tiny town far away in Kurland. Chertkov moved to England, where he supervised the publication of those of Tolstoy's works which had been banned in Russia.

Tolstoy, journeying to St. Petersburg to bid his disciples goodbye, grieved that these and other good men were being sent away for following his ideas. Why did the authorities not punish him too? From the capital Tolstoy informed some of his followers:

> You probably know that Chertkov and Biryukov have been sent into exile. . . . The sad thing is that they [the government] won't lay a finger on me. They are defeating their own purpose, however, for by leaving me free to speak the truth, they are compelling me to speak it.

After the intimate time of the famine relief work, Sonya's animosity to her husband's religious ideas flared up again. Hysteria often overcame her. She nagged and harried him. She objected to his work, to his followers, and even to the way he dressed. Sometimes she definitely seemed to be mentally ill. She threatened suicide over and over. Swollen with resentment, she would sometimes fling herself out-of-doors in freezing weather and hide in a ditch while the entire household searched for her.

129

When she was well again, she still begged her husband not to continue irritating the administration on behalf of the Dukhobors. She was afraid her own family might be deported. But Tolstoy continued his petitions to the Tsar.

During this time another tragedy was occurring. In primitive Samara, where the Tolstoy family had often visited and had an estate, a religious sect called the Molokhans was called upon by soldiers representing the bishop. The children in each Molokhan home were seized and forced into orphanages, on the grounds that they should be trained according to the Orthodox Church. At last the parents appealed to Tolstoy.

The believer in nonviolence objected violently. Tolstoy again wrote to Nicholas II, protesting, "For the love of God . . . these religious persecutions, which are causing the shame of Russia, must cease; the exiles must be sent back to their homes, the prisoners released, the children returned to their parents. . . ." There was no reply. A second appeal was also ignored. Then Tolstoy sent letters to the newspapers, attempting to sway public opinion in favor of the abused. He begged an influential friend to bring some pressure to bear on behalf of the Molokhans, saying, "It is impossible to remain calm when such evil actions are committed before your eyes. I am ashamed to belong to a people that stands for such things." Nothing helped.

At last Tolstoy's daughter Tanya managed to obtain an audience with one of the Tsar's ministers. To her surprise he listened carefully to her descriptions of the children who had been kidnapped by the Church. "The Bishop of Samara has gone too far," the minister admitted. "I shall write to the governor right away." Tanya sped the news to her astonished father. And the Molokhans' children were returned to their thankful parents.

The government made an amazing concession for the Dukhobors too. The sect was given permission to settle on uncleared land in Canada, far from the clutches of the Tsar and the Orthodox Church. Money was needed, however, to resettle these 7,000 Christians who waited now for freedom. Tolstoy appealed to the charity of the public, as he had done during the famine. Against his principles he also wrote to twelve men known to be extremely wealthy. He collected an enormous sum but it was still inadequate to transport so many people nearly halfway around the globe. The writer had no funds of his own to give, but he had an able talent and a ready pen. Among his papers he found the first draft of a story: *Resurrection* was rich with possibilities. With vigor he hurriedly rewrote this forceful work, which incorporated many of his philosophical ideas. He sent his son Sergei to England to discuss publication with Chertkov. All the profits were to go to the emigration expenses of the Dukhobor refugees. Sonya could hardly believe the fantastic sum her husband received for *Resurrection*. Though she disapproved the book's shocking indictment of the Orthodox Church, she, their daughters, and several friends pitched in to accomplish the copying. Publication began in the spring of 1899, and the money from the sale of the novel was used for its intended purpose. In a modern version of the move of the seventeenth-century Pilgrims, the Dukhobors embarked on their mass exodus to live and worship in freedom in the new world. The Quakers in England helped them, but the move was financed mostly by the efforts of one dedicated man. Sergei had made the plans for the embarkation and he accompanied the group to Canada. An affectionate letter from his father reached him in England: "Thank you, dear Sergei, for your readiness to serve the cause of the Dukhobors and—I know it—mine as well. I appreciate it greatly and think of you with joy. . . . L.T."

Tolstoy seldom seemed to find such pleasure in his children anymore. His son Leo was an outspoken critic of Tolstoy's ideas. Ilya and Sergei had married long ago and moved to their own estates. Tolstoy had not minded that somehow, but the marriages of Tanya and Masha had upset him. His two younger sons, Michael and Andrey, soon joined the army. This, of course, cruelly offended their father's anti-war principles, as well as his pride.

Finally the raw, unusual novel *Resurrection* reached the bookstores. Almost every literate Russian read it. In spite of the censor's scissors the story left no doubt in the reader's mind that the poor were constantly exploited by those in power. The Church was accused along with the State. A tremendous audience had been captured for Tolstoy's message: In Russia the "many" suffer daily while the privileged "few" lead idle, luxurious lives.

For years the officials of the Orthodox Church and the tsarist government had watched the momentum of the Tolstoyan movement. Since the famine, priests had followed orders to preach against this popular leader. Despite Tolstoy's unceasing efforts to express his doctrine of nonviolence, the government feared that he might try to achieve freedom and reform by uniting the millions of oppressed people in a revolution. With the publication of *Resurrection,* it seemed that this time Tolstoy had gone too far. An official met with the Holy Synod. He acknowledged his fear that either exiling or imprisoning Tolstoy might set off a popular revolt. Still, some action must be taken against him. He reminded the Synod that the Church had an ancient weapon— excommunication. The decision was made to excommunicate the people's prophet.

On February 24, 1901, an official decree was to be posted on the door of every church in Russia, proclaiming, "God has permitted a new false prophet to appear in our midst today, Count Leo Tolstoy." It continued, accusing the "world-famous author" of daring "to oppose God," and it ended by affirming, "Therefore the Church no longer recognizes him among her children. . . ." The nation responded to this excommunication strangely. Thousands rallied to Tolstoy's defense. Protests were heard not only from the writer's admirers and disciples, but from those who had never approved of his doctrines. Students took the opportunity to demonstrate for reform of the unfair military draft law and other injustices as well. Moscow was filled with unrest.

On the Sunday the decree appeared, Tolstoy was driving through the city after a visit to his doctor. Near Lubyanka Square the excommunicate was recognized by a crowd of anti-government demonstrators, mostly young people. "Hurrah for Leo Nikolayevich!" one dissenter shouted, using Tolstoy's family name.

"Long live Leo Nikolayevich!" proclaimed another.

Then the chanting outcry was taken up, "Hail to the great!" A tremendous throng of admirers surrounded his sledge and would not allow it to budge. Over and over came the refrain, "Hurrah! Hurrah! Hail to the great!" At last a policeman cleared a path to let the delighted old man pass through the crowd. The shouts rang through the frosty air and brought tears to his eyes as Tolstoy was carried on his way.

For weeks, telegrams, letters, and visitors poured into the Tolstoy family's Moscow home. Well-wishers sent flowers and messages bearing hundreds of signatures. An almost festive air prevailed. It seemed as though all Russia were reassuring her favorite citizen. We the Russian people love you and believe in you. There were also some anonymous threats on his life. His books were banned in a few libraries. The Moscow Temperance Society dropped him from its membership.

In April Tolstoy decided to reply to the excommunication decree with a simple article of faith. He remembered his despair and then the exquisite peace of his search for God. He felt within his soul that God required nothing but the truth. And he determined to answer the slanderous accusation of the Church.

"I believe in God, . . ." he affirmed. "I believe that the will of God is most clearly and intelligibly expressed in the teaching of the man Jesus. . . . I believe that man's true welfare lies in fulfilling God's will, and His will is that men should love one another. . . ." He described the Kingdom of God as "an order of life in which the discord, deception, and violence that now rule will be replaced by free accord, by truth, and by the brotherly love of one for another." Behind her mother's back young Sasha helped hectograph copies of this credo. It circulated rapidly through Moscow and was reprinted in newspapers around the world. When Tolstoy's statement of faith became public, there was a new wave of tribute to him. The Russians were basically a religious people, but many had also become disillusioned with the Orthodox Church. They did not fear Tolstoy as a "false prophet"; they admired him as a devout and truthful man of courage.

Bolstered and emboldened by the public response, Tolstoy published an appeal to the Tsar, suggesting fundamental government reforms to ease the oppression of the people: freedom of religion; education opportunities for the underprivileged; equal treatment in courts of law; equal rights for peasants.

"Such," he concluded, "are the modest . . . desires, we believe, of the immense majority of the Russian people." Tolstoy spoke for millions, for these reforms were also among the aims of the later revolt in 1905 and of the Russian Revolution of 1917. But Tolstoy could never have approved of the later violence. He was trying to achieve a free society by peaceful means. In his letter to the Tsar he added sincerely, "Only if this [reform] is done can your position be safe and really strong." The plea was not answered.

The manager of the *New Times*, Alexis Suvorin, jotted into his diary a note he would not have dared to use editorially:

> We have two tsars, Nicholas II and Leo Tolstoy. Which is the stronger? Nicholas II is powerless against Tolstoy and cannot make him tremble on his throne, whereas Tolstoy is incontestably shaking the throne of Nicholas II and his whole dynasty.

In the summer of 1901 the Tsar received the news that Tolstoy was ill with malaria. Perhaps Russia would soon be rid of this "second tsar." The police chiefs and governors of each province were ordered by telegram "to prevent any demonstrative speeches, activities, or public manifestations" in the event of Tolstoy's death.

But the illness subsided, and Tolstoy spent his seventy-third birthday in a violent dispute with his wife. Sonya had learned that while her husband was ill, he had discussed with Masha and signed a will which requested his family to make public their copyrights to his early works. Sonya furiously called her daughter a Pharisee and a hypocrite, then punished her husband with an endless tirade. Later she scrawled sadly but not unreasonably in her diary, "To make the works . . . *common* property I regard as wrong and senseless. I love my own family. . . . We shall only enrich the wealthy publishing houses. . . ."

Tolstoy, weary, had gestured that Sonya was to have her way, as usual. "The family is flesh," he said softly; ". . . for a pampered family more is needed. . . ." How he wished he could go far away to some peaceful place, to think, to pray, and later to die.

As though reading his mind, his doctors recommended relaxation in a warm climate. Soon Sonya, her husband, Sasha, blonde Masha and her husband, a few servants, and a doctor headed for the Crimea. Their destination was a beautiful borrowed villa in the winter sun. P. A. Boulanger, a Tolstoyan, had provided an elegant railroad car for the party. This was a change for the writer, who for years had traveled third class. He had to be carried aboard the train. Crowds gathered at stations along the way, calling, "Hurrah . . . Tolstoy! God protect you!" At Kharkov people shouted, "Tolstoy! Is he there? Here's a delegation! Let us come aboard! Hurrah! Tolstoy!" He waved feebly from the window of the train.

At Sevastopol, the old veteran rested a day. He insisted on being driven around the city as he reminisced about his army time. Visiting a war museum, he was disgusted with the miserable relics of the siege. "All this horror ought to be forgotten, . . ." he muttered. "It is terrible, terrible!"

The entire winter and spring were spent at Gaspra in the Crimea. Tolstoy was frequently visited by the authors Anton Chekhov and Maxim Gorky, and, to his surprise, the Grand Duke Nicholas, cousin of the Tsar. The invalid's health fluctuated. In January he developed a critical case of pneumonia. Doctors hurried down from St. Petersburg. Word flashed by telegraph that Tolstoy was again mortally ill. Officials continued to worry that his death might be followed by rebellions. His family hovered near, especially the loyal Sasha, who served as his faithful nurse. By spring, he had recovered again, and the family returned to Yasnaya Polyana. At Sonya's insistence, a doctor was invited to live at the house and serve as estate physician. Dr. Dushan Makovitsky had a short, pointed beard and a round, balding head. He had long been a Tolstoyan, and he reverenced his famous patient.

In 1903, Tolstoy was horrified to hear of a savage massacre of Jews in Kishinev. He had been stationed there for a while in 1854. A vivid picture of violence on streets he had strolled filled him with shame for Russia. He wrote bitterly to the Governor of Kishinev:

> Profoundly shocked by the atrocities committed at Kishinev, we extend our heartfelt sympathy to the innocent victims of mob savagery and express our horror at the acts of cruelty perpetrated by Russians, our scorn and disgust with all who have . . . allowed this dreadful crime to be committed.

Back at Yasnaya a tired old man continued his search for freedom on behalf of the poor and the innocent.

"SEARCH...ALWAYS KEEP... SEARCHING"

The Russo-Japanese War began without warning in January, 1904. Russia had gained authority in Manchuria and wanted extended powers in Korea. It was the old story of the icebound nation seeking warm-water ports. Japan also had ambitions in Korea and Manchuria. Japan feared Russia but was militarily well prepared, even anxious, to fight for control in the Far East. The Russian people had no heart for the war. It was thrust upon them by the corrupt tsarist government.

Tolstoy in anguish watched a reluctant army follow its leaders to the Far Eastern battleground. Everywhere men were illegally pressed into service. Recruiting officers worked in every village. Drunken draftees staggered aboard crowded troop trains which carried 30,000 men a month over the Trans-Siberian Railroad. The cook at Yasnaya Polyana was plucked from his kitchen and dispatched to the front. To his father's sorrow, Andrey Tolstoy volunteered for action.

A reporter from Philadelphia, Pennsylvania, cabled Tolstoy, asking him about the conflict. He replied:

> I am neither for Russia nor Japan, but for the
> working people of both countries, who have been
> deceived by their governments and forced to go to
> war against their own good, their conscience, and
> their religion.

And in a pamphlet called "Bethink Yourselves!" he declared,
"No one should fight."

Along with grim news and casualty lists from the Liaotung
Peninsula, where the war was being fought, the man of peace
received a sad blow from St. Petersburg. His cousin Alexandra
was dead. Granny was gone. The two had exchanged warm
letters only a few months before. Then in August his brother
Sergei died after cruel suffering from cancer of the tongue. As he
helped to lift his brother's casket, Tolstoy dolefully mused, "He
was proud of me, he would have liked to agree with me but he
could not. . . ." Dmitri. Nicholas. And now Sergei. Of the boys
who had searched for the green stick, only Leo remained. His
sister Marya, now an aging nun at the Shamardino Convent,
joined him briefly to mourn Sergei. Not long after, the Tolstoys'
second daughter died of pneumonia at the age of thirty-five. Her
father held her hand as life dwindled and ceased. This time he
did not ask "Why?" but "When?" and "Where?" It came to him
in that serious moment that real life is beyond time and space.

With the onslaught of the war Tolstoy's dream of a nation
dedicated to nonviolence suffered a great setback. The last
vestiges of his patriotism turned to bitterness and grief as Port
Arthur surrendered and Russia bowed in defeat to Japan.
Though stronger than her island conquerors, Russia in 1905 had
to make peace abroad in order to calm a new revolt at home.
"The revolution is in full swing," Tolstoy wrote sadly in his diary
on October 23, 1905. "There will be killings on both sides."
That year Russian peasants began to run wild, burning the
homes of the nobility. Army deserters were everywhere. Sailors
mutinied on the battleship *Potemkin*. There was a general strike
and fighting in the streets of many cities. Leon Trotsky had
become a powerful leader and was leading an uprising in St.
Petersburg. Workers marching in a protest toward the Tsar's

Winter Palace were halted by bullets. Hundreds died; at least a thousand were wounded. Tolstoy suffered at the thought of this slaughter. He condemned the revolutionary leaders:

> The crime committed at Petrograd [St. Petersburg] is horrible. . . . Dishonest agitators, for their own base ends, lead simple people to death. I do not blame the people, but I have not enough words to express my aversion for those who deceive them.

The nation's turmoil crushed his hopes. It seemed his search for peace had come to nothing. Finally the widespread violence was put down, with the government making a very few concessions. The Tsar promised an elected Duma or parliament; Tanya's husband, M. S. Sukhotin, later won election to it. But Tolstoy commented gloomily, "There is nothing in it for the people."

His own household was torn by strife. Sonya seemed determined to make a misery of her husband's last days. Or else she was mentally ill. It was difficult to tell whether or not her behavior was intentional. The question of Tolstoy's will and the disposition of his copyrights had become an obsession with her. She badgered him constantly and maliciously about these matters. The copyrights were also an obsession with him. He wanted to will them all to the public. He suffered strangely whenever he thought that anyone must pay money to buy his works. His wife had means enough of her own from the earlier publishing business, he reasoned. She and each of the children also had houses and extensive lands. Although Sonya had been advised that she had no legal hold on the posthumous rights to his works, she was determined that they all be left to her and her family. A publisher had already covertly offered her the unprecedented sum of one million rubles for permission to publish Tolstoy's complete works after his death.

Torturing her aging husband with a thousand reproaches on this subject, she sometimes threatened suicide, throwing the whole household into upheaval. These scenes increased as Tolstoy's health declined. He had suffered many small strokes, or "fainting spells," following his bout of illness in the Crimea. After each attack he lost his memory for a while, then recovered and seemed alert again. He still spent his mornings writing in his study. Visitors were received in the afternoon. He corresponded warmly with Mahatma Gandhi in India and with George Bernard Shaw in England. When William Jennings Bryan visited Yasnaya Polyana, he gave up an audience with the Tsar in order to spend an extra day in conversation with Tolstoy. In 1907 Thomas Edison sent the writer a dictaphone. Tolstoy was gratified to learn that the inventor had long been a vegetarian.

There were two thousand telegrams of congratulations on his eightieth birthday, along with many gifts and callers. The same year, 1908, Chertkov was allowed to return from exile in England. He built a house close to Yasnaya Polyana and visited the writer every day. When Tolstoy made him the guardian of his personal diaries, Sonya accused Chertkov of stealing them. She hated Chertkov and felt she, alone, should be her husband's editor. She was also acutely jealous of her husband's respect and affection for this stalwart Tolstoyan. "I shall kill Chertkov," she exploded one day. "I shall pay someone to poison him." In another deranged frenzy she seized a toy gun, an air pistol, and childishly shot a picture of Chertkov to pieces. Tolstoy tried to calm her fits of anger, which left them both exhausted. When her features were twisted with fury, he found himself looking in vain for the dreamy, girlish countenance, the dear face he had loved for so long. Now he pitied her, but he also longed for peace.

In 1909 the prophet of nonviolence was invited to attend the World Congress of Peace in Stockholm. Sonya threatened to poison herself if he went, so he declined the invitation. For Tolstoy there was neither world peace nor personal peace.

In his copious mail the unworldly thinker often found letters accusing him of living luxuriously, of saying one thing and doing another. If only those critics knew the ironic chaos of his "luxurious" life! His dream of a solitary existence in a simple peasant's hut returned to tempt him. But he told Sergei, "I am too feeble and too old to begin a new life."

Sasha, the youngest child, still lived at home. Each day she typed her adored father's manuscripts in the "Remington Room." This unpretentious, homely girl could hardly forgive her mother for the hostile, unbearably depressing atmosphere she created. She wished she could protect her tired Papa from Sonya's relentless tirades, and begged her brothers and sister to come and see for themselves how painful the situation had become. When they did appear, everyone took sides. The four younger sons, influenced by their mother, stood against Tolstoy. Sergei tried to stay neutral, as did Tanya. But noting her father's drastic fatigue, the older daughter urged Sonya to think of others, not just of herself. At this time the disposition of Tolstoy's diaries was bothering the unhappy woman. The thought that her husband's frank descriptions of their quarrels and the stories of his bachelorhood might be made public after his death was terrible. What shame that would be for her and the children! She kept shouting, "I shall kill myself, I shall take poison if he does not will the diaries to me! . . ." And she moaned repeatedly, "I am exhausted, I am ill, they have drawn all my strength from me."

Tolstoy insisted that he loved her and that he would make any concession to her, but that they must lead a more peaceful life. "My dear," he said, "stop tormenting . . . yourself, because you are suffering a hundred times as much as the others." Sonya refused to listen to him, but she did ask that a psychiatrist be called from Moscow. Dr. Dushan Makovitsky was still physician-in-residence at Yasnaya Polyana, but he had been there so long and was so much a Tolstoyan that Sonya had little respect for his opinion or advice. Two visiting doctors came and diagnosed her disease as extreme hysteria and paranoia. Dr. Dmitri Nikitin also examined Tolstoy's heart and found it very weak. The doctors advised the children that their elderly parents should live apart. This brought on a fresh whirlwind of protest from Sonya. And Tolstoy confided to Sasha, "I wish for death so much! It is the only release. Life is such a burden to me!"

In her diary Tanya recorded, "Mama had a very bad hysterical attack . . . and has worn down everyone around her. . . . We onlookers have the impression that she could easily put a stop to all the tragicomedy she is producing. . . ." Although she sympathized with her troubled father, Tanya could not stay to shield him. She had her young daughter and husband to take care of at home. So Tolstoy turned to faithful Sasha in his final ordeal.

For years he had dreamed that his copyrights would finally belong to the people. Now he decided that Sasha was the one to manage it for him. He had already told her privately of the plan to will his works to the public. But the legality of such an instrument was in question. One July morning he said to his youngest as she came into his study, "You know, Sasha, I have decided to make the will in your name only." When the girl spoke her doubts about handling such a responsibility, he answered, "I have decided on it. You are the only one who has stayed here with me, and it is quite natural that I should place you in charge. . . ." She understood that she was to renounce the rights after his death, making them common property.

Only once more did he mention the matter to her. After he had gone to bed one night he called to her through the closed door of his room, "Sasha!"

"Yes, Papa?"

"I wanted to tell you about the will. . . . It would be well to buy Yasnaya Polyana from Mama and your brothers and give it to the peasants. . . ."

"Very well, Papa." She would have marched through fire if those had been his orders.

Because of Sonya's fierce opposition to Tolstoy's will, it was signed secretly in the forest. Chertkov and three other friends and advisors assisted. Tolstoy felt strained and depressed. Several days later, with uncanny instinct, Sonya guessed that a will had been signed. In a blind rage she confronted her husband. He refused to answer. In the weeks that followed she made his life intolerable. She blamed Chertkov for everything and declared she was taking steps to have him banished again. Whenever he visited Tolstoy, Sonya spied and eavesdropped, hurling endless ridiculous accusations. There were constant tears and tension.

Awakened late one night by a noise in his room, Tolstoy found his wife wandering about in her nightgown, her hair wild and disheveled. Seeing his eyes open, she hastily left. He was choking, unable to sleep. What he had preached was a life of love

142

and simplicity. What surrounded him was misery and unhappy relationships in the guise of wealth and fame. Was it too late to change all that? Lying in bed, the eighty-two-year-old man reached a decision in the pre-dawn hours of October 28, 1910.

He rose quietly, lit a candle, and called softly to Dr. Makovitsky and to Sasha. He explained his plans to these two helpers. He packed a bag, wrote a letter to his wife, and left the house in which he had been born. "Where to go? Where to go, the farthest possible?" he asked the sleepy doctor, as they climbed aboard the second-class coach in the Shchekino railway station.

A great feeling of pity for Sonya came over him. "I'm sorry for her." He went out on the coach platform. As the train gathered speed, the doctor finally persuaded him to come in out of the freezing wind.

When Sonya realized that her husband had at last run away, she rushed out screaming and threw herself into the icy water of the carp pond. Sasha pulled her to safety. "Wire your father that I drowned myself," she sobbed. The girl tried to calm her mother. When they were warm and dry again, Sasha handed Sonya the letter from Tolstoy:

> My departure will grieve you. I am sorry for that, but . . . my position in the house . . . has become unbearable. . . . I beg you to forgive me for anything in which I have been at fault toward you, as I with all my soul forgive you for any wrong you have done me.

The distraught woman beat at herself with scissors, shouting, "I'll find him. . . . I'll jump out the window. . . . Just let me find out where he is and I'll never let him go again! . . . I'll lie down in the doorway! . . ." A doctor was called. He pronounced Sonya hysterical but not insane. At last her sons and Tanya arrived to console her. By turns she threatened, repented, accused, and refused to eat.

Sasha had promised her father not to reveal where he was staying. But she agreed to deliver the family's letters to him. All wrote urging him to return, except Sergei, who said, "The situa-

tion was hopeless and I think you chose the best way out." Sasha left that night.

She found her father at the Shamardino Convent visiting affectionately with his sister, Marya. That day he and Dr. Makovitsky had already looked in the area for a peasant's isba where he might live. When Sasha told him of Sonya's response to his leaving, he moaned, "If anything were to happen to her I should be very, very unhappy." He opened the letter from his wife:

> Lyovotchka, darling, come home and save me, dear, from a second attempt at suicide. . . . I will renounce all luxury entirely; I'll be friendly with your friends; I'll cure myself; I'll be kind. . . . Even the Gospel says you can never, in *any circumstances*, desert your wife. . . .

He felt a great weight. Asking to be left alone, he replied to Sonya's letter:

> Do not think that I have gone because I do not love you. I love you and pity you with all my heart—but cannot do otherwise than I am doing. . . . What matters is not the fulfillment of any . . . demands of mine, but only your . . . calm, rational attitude toward life. And as long as these are lacking, life with you is unthinkable to me. To return to you while you are in such a state would mean, for me, to renounce life. And I do not consider that I have the right to do so.
>
> Farewell, dear Sonya. God help you. Life is no jesting matter and we have no right to abandon it of our own will. . . . Perhaps those months which remain to us are more important than all the years we have lived, and they must be lived well.
>
> L. T.

He tried to sleep that night, but tossed restlessly. Sonya, his sons, even Tanya, might appear at any moment and carry him back. He must hurry away again. Early the next morning he, the doctor, and Sasha boarded a train in the darkness. Their destination was undecided. Newspapers brought aboard the coach proclaimed that Leo Tolstoy had made a sudden departure from Yasnaya Polyana. "They know everything already," Tolstoy muttered hoarsely.

Several passengers guessed his identity and passed the word that their traveling companion was none other than the world-famous friend of the oppressed. There were reactions of love, respect, and awe.

It was learned that a plainclothes policeman had come aboard at one of the stops and was observing the little group of runaways. Tolstoy complained of feeling chilly. He asked Sasha to tuck a steamer rug around him. His teeth were chattering. The doctor took his pulse, noting that he had a fever. They decided that he should be put to bed at the next station, the village of Astapovo.

On November 2, the worried family at Yasnaya Polyana received a telegram from a stranger: "Leo Nikolayevich ill at Astapovo. Temperature 104." They left for Astapovo as soon as they could on a special train.

Tolstoy was lying in a small, dingy bedroom in the station-master's house near the railroad. When the family arrived, Sasha and Dr. Makovitsky wondered how they could keep Sonya from bothering the patient. It was Sergei who said firmly, "Mama must not be allowed to see Father. It would excite him too much." She was installed in a private railway sleeping car parked on a siding. Outside the door of the little house, friends, reporters, photographers, curiosity seekers, and peasants milled about.

In the trying days that followed, the Tolstoy children, one by one, managed to slip in and speak to their dying father. Sergei's presence left Tolstoy quietly weeping for joy. "He . . . he kissed my hand!" Tears stood in his old eyes. Flushed with fever, breathing with great difficulty, he wanted to dictate a few thoughts. Sasha jotted the words into his ever-present diary. "God is that unlimited Whole of which man is a limited part. Only God truly exists. . . ." His voice trailed away. Strange, colorful delirium seemed to interrupt his rest as he lay in a fever for two days. Was he still searching for God? Or did he dream he was a young man again in Moscow, his arm in a sling, dictating to young Tanya Behrs, as he searched for words for an epic?

When his own Tanya tiptoed into the sickroom, her father asked haltingly about Sonya. "Perhaps you had better not talk, Papa, you get excited," she said, smoothing his pillow.

"Tell me! Tell me! What can be more important to me than that?" he insisted. Tanya reassured him and departed nervously.

His wife sat in the train, too weary to cry anymore. She started in fright each time one of her children returned from the stationmaster's cottage. "Does he know that I tried to drown myself?" she asked Sasha.

"Yes, he does."

"Wherever he goes, I will go," she repeated several times. Then she began another outburst of abuse against her husband. She reproached them all every day for imprisoning her. "You are keeping me from him," she said peevishly. ". . . At least let people believe that I have been with him." Meanwhile she talked continuously to reporters, policemen, and friends, condemning everyone for the outrageous way she was being treated.

On November 4 Tolstoy lapsed into unconsciousness. His hand was busy with an imaginary pencil, writing on the bedcovers. Once he murmured something unintelligible. Sasha bent over his moving lips.

"Search," he whispered, "always . . . keep . . . searching."

An official of the Orthodox Church arrived in Astapovo to make the gesture of inviting the excommunicated black sheep back into the fold. But the patient was not told of his visit. He slept fitfully during the next two days as his condition grew worse. His wrinkled hand continued to move across the blanket. The doctors were administering oxygen. The children hovered near the door. Suddenly he opened his eyes wide and called sharply, "Sergei!" The oldest son rushed to kneel beside his father's bed. Tolstoy's eyes looked for a last understanding as he moved his lips with difficulty. "Truth . . . I love much." Those incoherent phrases were his last words. His head fell back upon the pillows; he was unconscious.

In the chill of midnight on November 6, the sons supported

their mother across the railroad yard to the room where her husband lay. She whimpered when she saw the closed eyes in the familiar face and heard the agonized breathing. Kissing his pale forehead, she knelt beside the bed and murmured, "Forgive me, forgive me." Outside the little cottage, the crowds grew, while the life inside ebbed away. On November 7, 1910, at six in the morning, Tolstoy died.

Reporters at Astapovo telegraphed the news to the waiting world. Anxious officials alerted police throughout Russia: No demonstrations were to be allowed; no religious services; and no special trains would be permitted to leave for Yasnaya, except the one carrying the plain wooden coffin and the Tolstoy family. Nevertheless, at Astapovo and at every station along the way crowds paid final tribute to Tolstoy. Workingmen and nobles waited side by side in the cold, holding up their children to see the train carrying the body of the great Russian. At Yasnaya, a procession of mourners miles long—family, friends, and peasants—followed the coffin singing hymns, as they carried Tolstoy to the forest ravine, the place of the "green stick" of his childhood game. Here, according to his request, they buried him.

When the crowds left, the ravine was still and silent. No children played nearby. The air was cold. The trees had lost their leaves. Only the new grave remained, a mound of earth in the still woods. The dreamer was dead. His search was over. But the stories he told live on. And his dream of peace and of man's sincere search for truth, for freedom, and for God are not over.

In the winter of 1917, the Russian people's demand for freedom and reform burst into revolution. Tsar Nicholas II was forced to abdicate, and some months later he and his family were assassinated. All property owned by nobles was confiscated by the new government or was put to the torch by pillaging peasants.

Yasnaya Polyana became a State farm. In the beloved peacemaker's mansion Bolshevik soldiers were quartered, although the family was allowed to remain until Countess Sonya Tolstoy's death in 1919. The Tolstoy home in Moscow was also seized. After several years it became a museum memorializing the writer. Later the name of the little station where he had died was changed from Astapovo to Leo Tolstoy.

SUGGESTED READING:

WORKS BY LEO TOLSTOY

* Starred editions are available in paperback.

Anna Karenina. Edited by L. J. Kent and N. Berberova. Translated by Constance Garnett. Modern Library, Inc.

A Confession, The Gospel in Brief, and *What I Believe.* Translated and introduced by Aylmer Maude. Oxford University Press, Inc.

Childhood, Boyhood, and *Youth.* Translated by Michael Scammell. McGraw-Hill Book Company.

Fables and Fairy Tales. Translated by Ann Dunnigan. New American Library.

Great Short Works of Leo Tolstoy. (Includes: *Family Happiness, The Cossacks, The Death of Ivan Ilych, The Devil, The Kreutzer Sonata, Master and Man, Father Sergius, Hadji Murad, Alyosha the Pot.*) Harper & Row, Publishers, Inc.

Ivan the Fool and Other Tales of Leo Tolstoy. Translated by G. Daniels. Macmillan Company.

The Kingdom of God and *Peace Essays.* Translated by Aylmer Maude. Oxford University Press, Inc.

The Law of Love and the Law of Violence. Translated by Mary K. Tolstoy. Holt, Rinehart, & Winston, Inc.

Nikolenka's Childhood. Translated by Aylmer Maude and Louise Maude. Pantheon Books.

Recollections and Essays. Translated by Aylmer Maude. Oxford University Press, Inc.

Resurrection. Translated by Vera Traill. New American Library.

Russian Stories and Legends. Translated by Aylmer Maude and Louise Maude. Pantheon Books.

The Snowstorm and Other Stories. Translated by Aylmer and Louise Maude. Oxford University Press, Inc.

Tolstoy's Writings on Civil Disobedience and Non-Violence. Translated by Aylmer Maude. New American Library.

Twenty-Three Tales. Translated by Aylmer and Louise Maude. Oxford University Press, Inc.

*_War and Peace_. Two volumes. Translated by Rosemary Edmonds, Penguin Books, Inc.

What Men Live By. Translated by Aylmer and Louise Maude. Flemming H. Revell Co.

NOTES ON SOURCES

All quoted material has been taken from the following books.

Of the numerous translations of Leo Tolstoy's works into English, I have relied heavily on Aylmer Maude's extensive translations. All quotations from the following works by Tolstoy appear in Aylmer Maude's *The Works of Leo Tolstoy*, Tolstoy Centenary Edition, 21 volumes, London, Oxford University Press, 1928–1937:

Anna Karenina
Bethink Yourselves!
A Confession, The Gospel in Brief, and *What I Believe*
The Memoirs of a Madman
Recollections
Sevastopol in December

Quotes throughout the book from *The Private Diary of Leo Tolstoy 1853–1857* come from the Aylmer and Louise Maude translation, New York, Doubleday & Page Co., 1927.

Most quotes from *Childhood, Boyhood*, and *Youth* come from the Michael Scammell translation, New York, McGraw-Hill Book Company, 1964.

Throughout, I have used these major biographies of Tolstoy as sources for quotation of primary documents:

Maude, Aylmer, *The Life of Tolstoy*, 2 vols., Tolstoy Centenary Edition, London, Oxford University Press, 1929–1937.

Simmons, Ernest J., *Leo Tolstoy*, Boston, Little, Brown & Co., 1946.

Troyat, Henri, *Leo Tolstoy*, translated from the French by Nancy Amphoux, New York, Dell Publishing Co., Inc., 1969.

I have also quoted many primary documents found in:

Biryukov, Paul, *Leo Tolstoy*, New York, Charles Scribner's Sons, 1911.

Kuzminskaya, Tatiana, *Tolstoy as I Knew Him*, translated by Nora Sigerist, New York, Macmillan Co., 1948.

Noyes, George Rapall, *Tolstoy*, New York, Dover Publications, Inc., 1968.

Sukhotin-Tolstoy, Countess Tatiana, *The Tolstoy Home, Diaries of Tatiana Tolstoy*, translated by Alec Brown, New York, AMS Press, Inc., 1966.

Tolstoy, Countess Alexandra, *Tolstoy, A Life of my Father*, translated by Elizabeth Hapgood, New York, Harper and Brothers, 1953.

Tolstoy, Countess Alexandra, *The Tragedy of Tolstoy*, translated by Elena Varneck, New Haven, Yale University Press, 1933.

Tolstoy, Leo, *Last Diaries*, translated by Lydia Weston-Kesich, New York, G. P. Putnam's Sons, 1960.

Tolstoy, Sergei, *Tolstoy Remembered by his Son*, translated by Moura Budberg, London, Weidenfeld & Nicholson, 1961.

Tolstoy, Sonya, *Diary of Tolstoy's Wife*, 1860–1891, translated by Alexander Werth, New York, Payson and Clark Ltd., 1929.

For background I consulted:

Clarkson, Jesse, *A History of Russia*, New York, Random House, Inc., 1961.

Dillon, E. J., *Count Leo Tolstoy*, London, Hutchinson, 1934.

Dole, N. H., *The Life of Lyof N. Tolstoy*, New York, T. Y. Crowell Co., 1911.

Leon, Derrick, *Tolstoy, His Life and Work*, London, Routledge, 1944.

Stephenson, Graham, *Russia From 1812 to 1849*, New York, Frederick A. Praeger, Inc., 1970.

Tolstoy, Ilya, *Tolstoy, My Father: Reminiscences*, translated by Ann Dunnigan, Chicago, Cowles Book Corp., 1971.

Tolstoy, Countess Sonya, *Countess Sonya's Later Diary, 1891–1897*, translated by Alexander Werth, New York, Payson and Clark, Ltd., 1929.

Waleffe, Pierre, *Leo Tolstoy*, translated by A. Negro, Editions Minerva, Genève, 1969.

INDEX

Format by Gloria Bressler
Set in 11 point Times Roman
Composed by American Book–Stratford Press
Printed by the Murray Printing Company
Bound by American Book–Stratford Press
HARPER & ROW, PUBLISHERS, INCORPORATED